The Open University

Business School

Book 3

An introduction to accounting and finance in business

Written and coordinated by Judy Day and Vira Krakhmal with input from Lorna Eller, Diane Preston, Paul Ranford and George Watson

The Open University Walton Hall, Milton Keynes MK7 6AA

First published 2006. Second edition 2009. Third edition 2010. Fourth edition 2011.

Edited and designed by The Open University.

Printed and bound in the United Kingdom by Charlesworth Press, Wakefield.

ISBN 978 1 8487 3652 8

4.1

Contents

Introduction to Book 3

Welcome to Book 3 of B120 *An introduction to accounting and finance in business*. We hope that you will find this book interesting and enjoyable. Today's students find studying accounting and finance increasingly relevant to the study of contemporary business. They are often reassured by the fact that the study of accounting and finance is less about maths and more about developing basic numeracy skills.

This book contains five study sessions designed to give you a thorough introduction to the use and importance of accounting and finance in business. Simple business examples are used throughout. Extra help with the ideas and activities presented in this book is provided in the B120 Book 3 Study Companion. Use of the Study Companion is intended to be an integral part of your study of Book 3 and is counted in your total study hours for this course. All accounting and finance concepts are introduced in **bold italic** text the first time that they are used in Book 3 and are then explained in the B120 Glossary.

Each study session is supported by learning activities. These should be seen as an integral part of your study: if you skip them or leave them until later you may find difficulty in understanding the next session. Each activity is followed by a feedback section. The activities will be most useful to you if you cover up the feedback section while you think about and complete each activity. For many activities we have not attempted to give 'model answers' but rather to offer an informed, experienced viewpoint that you may wish to consider. You may find as you progress through the book that you develop more considered answers to earlier questions. You may then find it worthwhile to return to the activities and annotate your previous answers. This will allow you to reflect on what you have learnt since you first completed each activity.

Our intention is not to teach you about the detailed technical aspects of doing accounts in a business. Rather, it is to provide an accessible introduction to the relevance of accounting to business and to make sure that you are aware of the key terms, rules and types of accounting that any business will have to contend with. Whether you know nothing or only a little about the subject, we feel sure that by the end of studying this book you will appreciate accounting as a key component of decision making within any type of business.

Aims and objectives

The aims of Book 3 are to:

- give you a good grounding in the fundamental terms, concepts and concerns of accounting and finance in business;
- raise your awareness of the relevance of accounting and finance to decision making in everyday business practice;
- describe the context in which accounting has developed and now operates;

- provide an understanding of the key components of accounting in a business, such as the basic accounting statements and budgets;
- begin to develop your knowledge of how spreadsheets are used in accounting and finance.

Structure

Book 3 is divided into five study sessions:

Session 1	introduces the need for businesses to account for what they do. We reflect on some of the main purpose of accounting in a business and think about the main users of financial information. For financial information to be of use to the business it needs to have certain characteristics, such as reliability and timeliness; these are also outlined in this first session. For interest, we explore how accounting began and then use the idea of a system and an organisational conversion process to help us understand more about how accounting operates in a business.
Session 2	begins by highlighting the differences between private and public entities in accounting terms. The small business example Paula's Pipes is introduced and then used throughout the book to explain accounting concepts. We reflect further on the different types of financial information that different financial stakeholders need, and then spend time introducing the concept of cash accounting, the accounting equation and principles of double-entry bookkeeping.
Session 3	outlines the three most important accounting statements for a business: the profit and loss account, the balance sheet and the cash flow statement. Several key accounting concepts are explained, such as cash forecasting, budgets, accrual accounting, assets, liabilities and equity, and are demonstrated through the accounts of our recurrent small business case, Paula's Pipes.
Session 4	thinks about the world in which accountancy and accountants operate. The conceptual framework of accounting is introduced and the concept of value is clarified. The different types and branches of accounting are described. Finally, the image of accountancy is considered and students are asked to prepare for a presentation exercise about accounting scandals.
Session 5	deals with the process of accounting that takes place within the business. If a business does not produce high-quality accounting information for internal use, then it is in danger of getting into financial difficulties. Budgetary control is explained using several simple business examples.

Session 1 What is accounting?

Why are we studying 'what is accounting?'? Accounting is crucial to the running of any business. It is concerned with the flow of economic resources in and out of the business and, more significantly, it is about providing information for decision making.

The **aims and objectives** of Session 1 are to:

- explore the main purposes of accounting;
- introduce the main users of accounting information;
- describe the characteristics of good financial information;
- outline the history and development of accounting;
- use the metaphors of system and conversion process to help make sense of what accounting is.

1.1 Why do we need accounting?

The word 'account' in everyday language is often used as a substitute for an explanation or a report of certain actions or events. As an employee, for example, you may need to account for how you have been spending your time, or as a manager you may need to account to the owners of the business you run as to whether, and why, the business has been making a *profit* or *loss*. As it is not always easy to remember every detail of what happens in the course of a year, you may well be keeping some sort of written record as you go along. Such records are, in effect, the basis of a simple accounting *system*.

At this very early point, let's spend a few minutes reflecting on the question: what is accounting about?

Activity 1.1

Spend about **10 minutes** on this activity

Purpose: to reflect on the main purposes of accounting in a business.

Task: jot down some key words or initial ideas in answer to the question: what do you think is the main purpose of accounting in a business?

Feedback

You may have found this question difficult, or perhaps you already have some idea or experience of accounting. You may have said that the main purpose of accounting is any one (or more) of the Items on the following list.

Accounting allows the business to know:

- if it is making a profit or a loss
- what it is worth
- what a transaction was worth
- how much cash it has

- how much money it is owed
- how much is owed to other people and businesses
- how to keep a financial check on things.

The list could go on and on. (You might have used slightly different terms – like 'surplus' and 'deficit' instead of 'profit' and 'loss'.) If you thought the main purpose of accounting in business was any of the items listed, you did well. They are all similar. However, the primary purpose of accounting can be summarised thus: to provide information for decision making.

The information is usually thought to be financial, but it need not be – it could be, for example, the number of sheep owned by a farmer, or the number of cars belonging to a car dealer, or the number of footballers under contract to a football club. Despite this, one common characteristic that information produced by accounting and accountants usually possesses is that it is capable of being turned into information expressed in financial terms.

Here's a basic definition of accounting for you to consider:

> Accounting is about the provision of financial information to help with decisions about resource allocation, and about the preparation of financial reports which describe the results of past resource allocation decisions.

Who are the people who need such information? We look at the different users in the next section.

1.2 The users and usefulness of financial information

One way of thinking about accounting is to regard it as a service function. The accounting process produces financial information for certain clients or users, as Figure 1.1 shows.

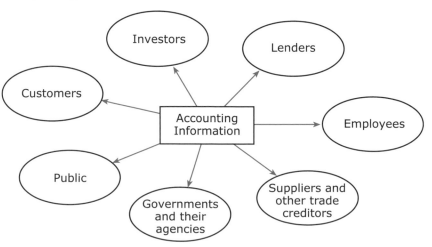

Figure 1.1 The main users of accounting information. (Source: Dyson, 2004, p. 9)

It can be suggested that the quality and nature of this service provided by accountants will be determined by the extent to which the information needs of the different users are met. It can also be argued that, in order to meet the needs of users, financial information should possess certain key characteristics. Atrill and McClaney (2001, p. 5) suggest that these are:

- relevance
- reliability
- comparability
- understandability.

The first two characteristics, they suggest, are really what makes information useful, while the other two will affect usefulness by the extent to which they are either present or missing. Atrill and McClaney also point out that these characteristics are sometimes in conflict with one another, so in practice it may be necessary to trade off one characteristic against another. They use the example below to illustrate this.

Example 1.1

[A] manager may require information on the current selling price of a unique cutting machine owned by the business in order to decide whether or not a recent offer for the machine should be accepted. Information concerning the current selling price is likely to be very relevant to the manager's decision but may not be very reliable, particularly as the machine is unique and there is likely to be little information available concerning market values.

(Source: Atrill and McClaney, 2004, p. 5)

At this point it is worth considering the characteristics of good financial information in more detail.

The characteristics of good financial information

- *Relevance* Information must be directly useful in the context of any decisions that need to be made. It can be argued that, for information to be useful, it should be capable of influencing the economic decisions of users. In other words: could possession of that information make a difference to users' views of the events or situation being described, and to their actions?
- *Reliability* Information should be free from deliberate error or bias. It should also accurately reflect the actual substance of events or transactions while taking a prudent view of them.
- *Comparability* Information should be prepared and presented in such a way that users can make valid comparisons both over time and between different organisations.
- *Understandability* Information should be comprehensible to reasonably well-informed users. This reflects the fact that users may need to be prepared to study the information and interpret it for their own purposes.

Some other points to bear in mind are:

- *Timeliness* Financial information should be available when needed. This characteristic has links to relevance, in that information that is not timely will not be capable of influencing the economic decisions of users.

- *Materiality* Is the information significant? One way of assessing this is to ask whether the inclusion, omission or misrepresentation of a piece of information would affect users' decisions. If it would not, because of its relative insignificance in the context being considered, it could be argued that this information should not be provided because it might simply prove to be a distraction. This would be the case however relevant and/or reliable that information might be. Clearly, materiality is context-driven: what is material for one situation or user may not be material in another context.

We might also want to consider whether the value provided by the information, in terms of better decision making, is greater than the costs of generating it. This can be thought of as an over-riding criterion.

Activity 1.2

Spend about **15 minutes** on this activity

Purpose: to reflect on the qualities of good financial information with the help of an example.

Task: read the scenario below and answer the question that follows it.

Imagine that you are Sue, who owns and runs a small local travel agency. Sue has just returned to work in January after the New Year break and has received a letter from her bank manager. In it he asks whether she can confirm that she will be able to repay the outstanding balance on a five-year loan that she took out four years ago to buy the business. The balance due is £10,000 and it is scheduled to be repaid by 31 December of the current year. Sue realises that she needs some financial information, so she asks Gavin, her office assistant, to help her.

Question: Describe the financial information that Gavin needs to find to help Sue reply to the bank manager.

Feedback

Gavin can help by giving Sue information on current and expected **income**, in the form of expected cash receipts, for the business, over the next twelve months. Sue will also need estimates of her **expenses**, in the form of expected cash costs of running the business. Comparison of the two will help Sue assess whether the business is likely to have enough in the bank to repay the loan by the end of the year. You might also have said that Sue needs to check on how much is currently available in the business's bank account.

Activity 1.3

Spend about **15 minutes** on this activity

Purpose: to further reflect on the qualities of good financial information.

Task: read the paragraph below, which describes a development in the scenario described in the previous activity, and then tackle the question that follows it.

Imagine that Gavin comes back to Sue with the following information: 'Good news! At the moment business is excellent and we are selling holidays worth around £10,000 a month in commission to us. But don't forget that this will only last until the end of April – by May we will be making only half that a month because most of our business over the summer relates to last-minute bookings, which tend to be discounted. Don't worry, though: once everyone is back at school and work at the end of the summer things pick up, and September to December should see business back to the same level as it is now.'

Sue thinks about this, and scribbles some figures on the back of an envelope. She reckons that the business's normal running expenses (which include Gavin's salary and interest on the loan) come to around £5,000 a month. She takes £2,500 a month for herself (and settles her own tax bill separately out of this). The only other expenses that she needs to remember are the business's ATOL (Air Travellers Organisers' Licensing) scheme membership fee and other insurance premiums. She normally pays these in August, and last year the total payable was £1,500.

Question: Can Sue repay the bank loan by the end of December? (You may need to use a simple calculator to help with this task.)

Feedback

We can present the financial information that Sue has collected like this:

		£	£
Income:	8 months @ £10,000		80,000
	4 months @ £5,000		20,000
			100,000
Expenses:	12 months @ £5,000	60,000	
Sue	12 months @ £2,500	30,000	
ATOL and insurance:	one-off @ £1,500	1,500	91,500
			8,500

So, these figures show that Sue can't quite repay the bank loan at the end of December, unless she already has at least £1,500 in her business bank account.

You might have prepared this information on a monthly basis. If you did, or were considering doing so, well done! We will see in later sessions that spreadsheets are very good for dealing with this type of presentation.

Now consider the financial information you have just prepared for Activity 1.3. Does it meet the criteria for good financial information that was discussed earlier? These were:

- relevance
- reliability
- comparability
- understandability
- timeliness
- materiality.

These are the comments we had on this question:

- *Relevance* The information prepared for Sue is highly relevant to her problem. It shows that she may not be able to repay the loan on the due date, so it will influence her economic decisions – and the bank manager's (assuming that she shows him the figures).
- *Reliability* We might be less certain about this. However, there is (as far as we know) no deliberate bias here, though there may be errors of judgement and estimation. We could advise Sue to be more prudent in her estimates. To accountants this would usually mean underestimating income, and overestimating expenses, to be on the safe side. For the purpose Sue has in mind we could argue that it is less important for the information to be reliable than it is for it to be relevant. Again,

spreadsheets have their uses here: we could use one to make changes in Sue's estimates and to assess the effect of these changes on the overall result.

- *Comparability* As long as Sue and Gavin have used the same basis in making their estimates, the figures should be comparable with those for previous years. The bank manager may wish to compare the figures with those of other clients in similar lines of business, and this may prove more of a problem as he may not know how these estimates have been made.

- *Understandability* The figures are easy to understand. They are presented simply and the calculations were not difficult.

- *Timeliness* The figures are timely. Sue didn't have to wait to get them, and they reflect the most up-to-date information that is available.

- *Materiality* The figures matter to Sue for the purpose for which she is preparing the information, and will have an effect on her decisions. For example, she now knows that she may not be able to repay the bank loan on the due date, and will have to decide how to deal with this situation.

A final question to think about with regard to the financial information suggested for Activities 1.2 and 1.3 is: does the value provided by the information exceed the costs of preparing it? Have a go at making notes on this question before reading the ideas provided below.

We would probably argue that the value provided for Sue by this information does exceed the (very low) costs of preparing it. However, if she had gone to an accountant for the information, she might have had to pay more than it was worth – and had to wait for it too.

We hope that this example of Sue's travel agency has made you start to see the importance and relevance of financial information to any type of business.

It is also important to realise that financial information is just one form of information. In order to run a successful business you need other information that is non-financial. Let's think about that now, using Activity 1.4 below.

Activity 1.4

Spend about **10 minutes** on this activity

Purpose: to reflect on the non-financial information required to run a business.

Task: think of a local business that you know fairly well, or perhaps one that you have worked (or work) for. What non-financial information can you think of that might be needed by this business to ensure its success? Make a list of your ideas before looking at the feedback section below.

Feedback

A number of responses to this task might be appropriate. The following is a list of just some of the non-financial information that might be crucial to protect and develop the business:

- customer satisfaction

- customer complaints
- health and safety standards
- strategy of competing businesses
- employee turnover
- employee satisfaction
- market share
- government policy
- local government planning regulations.

Having got to grips with some definitions and aspects of financial information, we can now stand back and consider what originally gave rise to accounting within businesses.

1.3 How accounting began

Accounting has been going on for thousands of years. Basically, every business needs to know how much it has sold and how much it has purchased, what cash has been received and paid, how much it owes and is owing to it, and whether it is making a profit (where the income is greater than the expenses) or loss (where the expenses are greater than the income) over a particular time period.

In earlier times, even these basic pieces of data might not have been formally recorded. Rather, only the *invoices* (each of which shows the details of a transaction) and *receipts* (each of which confirms that a payment has been made) would have been kept, in order to calculate the profit or loss of the business up to that point. Quite often it would have been the owner of the business who performed all these tasks. As businesses grew in size, however, it became less common for the owner to personally maintain the accounting records and more usual for someone to be employed as an accounts clerk. Then, as businesses grew even more, managers frequently became separated from the legal owners of the business, with the latter often having no involvement in the day-to-day running of the business. This led to a need for some monitoring of the managers. Checking of the financial records by professional accountants (this is known as *auditing*) became the norm and this, effectively, established the accounting profession.

The next example shows us something about the centrality of accounting to economic success even at a national level.

Example 1.2

In the sixteenth century the drive to explore Central and South America was of huge political significance to Spain. It was also expected to be of huge economic significance because of the gold and silver which the Spanish knew existed there, as they could see in the ornaments of the Aztecs and the Incas, for instance. In conquering South America, Spain expected not only to recoup the financial losses it had incurred from a serious of financially disastrous wars which had been waged by Emperor Charles V and later his son Philip II, but also to become rich. The Aztec treasury fell to the Spanish in 1513 and the Inca treasury in 1533. Their gold and silver mines were soon found too. During this period, Spain was experiencing a military and political boom.

But the monarchs of that time did not understand accounts and had no notion of the financial practices being developed in Italy in the mid-fifteenth century by prosperous merchants and cautious bankers. When the Jews were expelled from Spain in 1492, the country lost thousands of merchants and financial experts and the skills they specialised in were despised.

No one knew – or seriously asked – how much it really cost to build, equip and arm the fleets necessary to transport the conquerors (Conquistadors) and their troops from and to Spain, or how much it cost to build the towns, cities, roads and great religious temples needed to accommodate the physical and spiritual needs of conquerors and conquered. In addition, the costs of importing slaves to increase the labour forces working the mines and carrying out structural works, of paying indigenous labour and of equipping ports and escorting precious metals back to Spain were never calculated. Neither did anyone estimate the cost of piracy (the English seized a good deal of the precious metals on their way back to Spain).

The Incas, however, had a sophisticated accounting device: the *quipu*. A simple *quipu* is a string with knots used to record thousands, hundreds and tens. Large and sophisticated *quipus* could hold very complex sets of accounts. The Aztecs also kept sophisticated accounts. Early explorers made use of these, but later these skills were lost amid the push to eradicate indigenous beliefs and customs and to convert the 'Indians' to Christianity. Spain was spiralling into greater and greater fiscal problems and debt while, at the same time, the Conquistadors were busily burning the accounting methods of the Aztecs and the Incas.

Spain's poor economic vision created a conundrum which is still discussed today. Despite the shiploads of silver and gold transferred from America's mines and the Aztec and Inca treasuries to Spain, the country underwent five economic collapses: in 1595, 1607, 1627, 1647 and 1656. The conquest of Latin America brought Spain economically to its knees; just as the Spanish empire was rising politically it was sinking economically because of its failure to understand cost accounting.

(Source: adapted from Montaner, 2000, pp. 117–21; Jacobsen, 1964, pp. 221–8)

Accounting has expanded greatly from its informal beginnings. For large businesses in particular, its outputs are now heavily regulated and controlled and there are well-established procedures for virtually all the traditional accounting tasks.

The day-to-day environment within which accounting processes exist is known as the *accounting information system* (often abbreviated to 'accounting system'). We explore accounting information systems in the next section.

1.4 Accounting information systems

A system can be defined as a group of elements that are formed and interact in order to achieve goals or objectives. Life is full of systems – home, work, family, school, etc. A business is a system in which a number of people work together to achieve particular objectives. Within each system there are smaller systems. Within a business there are sub-systems called departments or functions which can themselves be broken down into smaller systems, right down to the level of individual employees.

All systems are located within an external environment. A business receives inputs to its system in the form of raw materials from suppliers, payments from customers, etc. It then converts these inputs into goods and services and sends its outputs (goods and services) into its external environment (to its customers). It records these activities in its accounting information system.

Figure 1.2 shows examples of the data inputs and information outputs from an accounting information system.

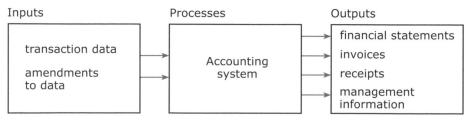

Figure 1.2 A simple accounting information system

Businesses continue to exist because managers take decisions about what they should do. In order to take a decision, a manager needs information. The information is provided to the manager from an information system. It is an item of output from the information system. Any decision taken by the manager is input back into the information system. Changes are then made to the information held within the information system, and then output from the information system to the recipient(s) – sometimes as regular reports, sometimes on demand.

For example, a manager who is in charge of ordering raw materials will be told by the information system how much raw material is held by the business and how much will now be needed. The manager then decides how much raw material to order and who to order it from. That decision is entered into the information system by the manager, the order is sent to the supplier by the information system and the information system is updated to show that an order has been placed.

Businesses have a number of systems – purchasing, production, marketing, human resources, and so on. They also have a general information system. This information system receives data from its external environment, processes it, and then sends the converted data into its external environment in the form of information. The accounting system is just one of the systems within a business, all of which must work together in an effective and efficient way. The accounting information system is part of the business's general information system. Whereas the general information system will process a mixture of quantitative (i.e. numerical) and qualitative (i.e. non-numerical) data, the accounting information system focuses almost entirely on processing quantitative data, usually expressed in monetary values.

1.5 Accounting as an organisational resource conversion process

One characteristic that all businesses share, irrespective of the sector or activity they are involved in, is the fact that they take in resources from the external environment, process them and then deliver outputs which have greater value than the original inputs. Capon (2004, p. 7) suggests that the processes to which the inputs are subjected can be described as an 'organisational resource conversion process'. This process can be observed in both service and manufacturing sectors and in the private, public and voluntary sectors. The resource conversion process can be represented as a chart containing a sequential list of inputs, conversion processes and consequent outputs. There are also three kinds of inputs, processes and outputs: human, tangible, and intangible. These are shown in Table 1.1.

This chart can be adapted and applied to individual businesses according to their particular context. It must be recognised that while inputs, processes and outputs are shown as separate elements in the conversion model, they should not be considered as independent of each other. For example, there can be no outputs if there are no conversion processes, and the processes cannot operate without inputs.

Table 1.1 Organisational resource conversion chart

	Resource inputs	Processes	Outputs
Human	• Owners/shareholders • Managers • Employees • Part-timers • Contractors	• Goal setting • Decision making • Planning products and services • Managing functions (including HRM) • Assembling parts • Manufacturing goods • Dealing with customers	• Job satisfaction or dissatisfaction • Salaries and wages • Bonuses and/or profit shares • Satisfied or dissatisfied customers
Tangibles	• Money (loans, overdrafts, profits, private capital) • Buildings • Machines and equipment • Raw materials • Components • Energy (gas, water, electricity) • Market research data	• Assembly • Manufacture • Service delivery • Supply • Quality control • Accounting • Distribution • Formal communication systems • Formal information systems	• Products • Services • Waste materials • Waste energy • Effluent • Accounting reports • Profit or loss
Intangibles	• Systems • Design • Information • Innovation	• Informal communication • Culture • Corporate memory • Informal information flow	• Professionalism • Happiness • Image and reputation • Innovation

(Source: adapted from Capon, 2004, p. 7)

Table 1.1 helps to show that the accounting information system is just one element of the organisational resource conversion process. However, it is an extremely important element, and most businesses could not manage properly without it. Think back to the example of Sue's travel agency in Activities 1.2 and 1.3. We do not know any details about the accounting information system in her business, but clearly there must have been some sort of system in operation, otherwise she and Gavin would not have been able to produce the figures they needed. Accounting information systems, like other elements of the organisational resource conversion process, are adaptable and can be tailored to suit the size, nature and needs of the individual business. Another way of putting this is to say that the specific design of an accounting information system is contingent upon the requirements of the business concerned, and upon that business's specific characteristics.

1.6 Conclusion

In this first study session we spent some time thinking about what accounting is and does within a business. We looked at the users of financial information and the characteristics of useful information. We explored the long history of accounting and where it came from. Finally, we used the ideas of a system and an organisational resources conversion process (Table 1.1) to help us think about what accounting does.

In the next study session we explain the two main types of business entities: sole traders and companies. We also start to explore some fundamental aspects of business accounts by using the example of a sole trader, a small business called Paula's Pipes.

1.7 Learning outcomes

By the end of this study session you should be able to:

- offer a definition of what accounting is and why individuals and businesses do it;
- list the main users of financial information;
- define and explain the main characteristics of good or useful financial information;
- explain in basic terms how accounting has developed over time;
- illustrate the basis of the accounting function in business by using the concept of a system or resource conversion process.

You will have developed your learning by:

- thinking about how you could help the owner of a business (in this case, Sue's travel agency) to get together some basic financial information;
- reflecting on the beginnings and development of the accountancy profession.

Session 2 Businesses and cash accounting

Why are we studying 'businesses and cash accounting'? Accounting needs and requirements differ according to the size and type of business. It is important you understand at this early stage what these different types of businesses are called within an accounting context. The cash account is a simple record of cash coming in and going out through a business over a period of time and thus forms a key component of the accounting process.

The **aims and objectives** of Session 2 are to:

- differentiate between different types of business organisation and their accounting needs;
- introduce you to an example of a small business, Paula's Pipes;
- describe the different financial stakeholders who will take an interest in the accounts of a business;
- explain what a cash account is and how it is constructed.

2.1 Accounting in different types of business

In the last study session we looked at the nature and development of accounting and used the idea of a system and a resource conversion process to help you understand how accounting works in a business. At the start of this second session we need to acknowledge that the accounting process and its outputs might be slightly different in different types of business. We will use an essential reading taken from Dyson (2004), first, to clarify these differences and, second, to introduce some more key terms you will need to be familiar with when studying accounting.

Activity 2.1

Spend about **1 hour** on this activity

Purpose: to clarify the difference between private and public entities.

Task: read Essential Reading 1, 'Public and private entities' by John Dyson, which you will find at the back of this book. Make notes as you go along and then turn to the appropriate section of B120 Book 3 Study Companion for a set of questions that will test your understanding of this reading.

Feedback

We have not provided feedback for this activity because we want you to complete the reading. It is an essential reading for this book and study time has been allocated to it.

2.2 Paula's Pipes

In this section we introduce an example of a small business called Paula's Pipes.

Paula is an example of a sole trader in the commercial sector. She is a plumber trading as 'Paula's Pipes'. Why might Paula want to keep accounts? Quite a few sole traders might ask this question along the lines of 'as long as there is enough money in my bank account I don't need to bother too much about accounts, do I?' Of course you will have spotted that at least part of the answer to this question involves the tax authorities at HM Revenue and Customs (formerly the Inland Revenue).

Self-employed persons in the UK are required to make an annual tax return showing what they have earned. To make sure that tax is charged only on their profit they need to keep a record of their expenses – all the costs incurred in making that profit. Even for the simplest business, one person trading by themselves, records are needed to show how much came in to the business and how much went out.

So for the plumber, Paula, the accounts might consist of:

- charges paid by customers to Paula;
- less costs of materials from plumbers' merchant;
- less costs of her van;
- less administrative costs such as telephone calls, heating and rent.

This gives the profit figure that HM Revenue and Customs want to know about. Is this figure of any use to Paula herself? We would say, yes. Even at this very basic level it gives her an idea of how much she needs to charge to cover her costs and provide herself with an income. By combining that figure with her knowledge of the local going rate and the local demand for plumbing services Paula can estimate if the business is going to be sustainable.

So already there are two bodies interested in Paula's accounts: herself and HM Revenue and Customs (in the UK). If the business grows, more people will have an interest in it. Once the turnover exceeds the value added tax (VAT) threshold (£68,000 in 2009 in the UK) the business has to register for VAT, charge VAT on work done, keep specific records, make VAT returns and be inspected. The VAT people (another part of HM Revenue and Customs) are not interested in any profit made by Paula, but in the correct recording of VAT charged and paid.

In order to develop her business to the extent that she might exceed the VAT threshold, Paula may have to borrow money to buy further equipment or a new van. Assuming the money is borrowed from a bank, what will the bank's customer service manager want to know about the business? Different banks may have different approaches. They may want to see sets of accounts for previous years or a business plan showing how the new equipment will contribute to the business, or they may require the borrowing to be secured against Paula's house, or they may insist on some combination of these. What the bank is seeking is reassurance that its money is safe, that it will get paid the interest on the loan, and that if Paula's Pipes ceases trading the bank can get its loan back.

As the business grows, Paula will probably want a credit account with a plumbers' merchant. What will its credit controller want to know about Paula's business? Like the bank, the plumbers' merchant will want to know that it will get paid. So it is interested in Paula continuing to trade and having enough cash to be able to meet their trading terms.

For this growing sole trader we have identified five bodies that will take an interest in one aspect or another of her financial health and records. These are just some of the financial stakeholders who may be interested in a business.

2.3 Financial stakeholders

To introduce this section on financial stakeholders, we start with a short activity.

Activity 2.2

Spend about **15 minutes** on this activity

Purpose: to understand the variety of interested stakeholders of different types of business and their needs.

Task: for each business in the table below think of who is going to be interested in the accounts for that business, and enter them into the table. We have offered suggestions for a state secondary school as an example to get you started.

	Sector		
	Commercial	**Public**	**Not for profit**
1 person	Paula's Pipes	N/A	N/A
Small	Corner shop	Town library	Local museum
Medium	Small supermarket chain	State secondary school *government, head teacher, parents, suppliers, VAT people, bank*	Regional scouting group
Large	International chemical company	Hospital	International charity

Feedback

There are no right answers to this activity; it is intended to get you thinking about different types of business and stakeholder.

Your list probably includes many of the stakeholders identified for Paula's Pipes: HM Revenue and Customs, the bank and suppliers. In addition you will probably have suggested 'owners' of some kind – be they sole traders, partners or shareholders – for the commercial examples. These are people with a direct interest in the worth of the business, its ability to make profits, and the profits it generates.

Under the **public sector** organisations you may have thought of government (either central or local) as being interested in the accounts. In the not-for-profit examples you may have put trustees of a charity or members of the organisation. In both these categories you might also have used the terms 'electors' or 'citizens' or 'members of the public'. All these could be described as being 'owners' of the public or not-for-profit sector entities. However, compared with owners in the commercial sector they have a less direct interest in the worth of the business and any profits it makes. Their interest may be more concerned with looking for evidence that the business has provided what it was supposed to provide with the funds they contributed: for instance, the choir subscriptions have been spent on rental of halls for practice, donations for emergency relief have reached the disaster victims, council tax has been spent on books for libraries, or road repairs have been done.

So one reason for keeping accounts is to produce a report of what a business has done with money: either generating wealth from the owners' money or producing goods and services with tax payers' or subscribers' money. You may already see a problem emerging here: although money can measure profit or loss, it can only partially describe goods and services. So the accounting statements required may need to include more than just accounting figures.

In your answers to Activity 2.2 you may have suggested that customers are interested in the accounts of a business. If you ordered a custom-built kitchen you want the supplier to stay in business long enough to build it, deliver it and honour any guarantee. So you would be looking for accounts that indicate a strong financial position. Does this apply to all businesses? Reconsider the secondary school. There are private profit-making and charitable not-for-profit schools as well as schools funded by taxes. Although children are the users of school services it is parents who worry about which school is best for them. What do parents look for in a school? Let's take a couple of minutes to think about that now.

How many things will feature in the accounting statements of the school? Parents considering a fee-paying school or a school that asked for a lot of contributions to fund activities might be concerned whether they could afford to send their children there. Many things parents think about will not be financial. They may be to do with the quality of the school – its atmosphere, academic record, artistic or sporting achievements – or to do with the suitability of that school for the children in question. For instance: is it close by, do siblings go there, are their friends going there, do its areas of excellence match the child's interests and talents? There are figures that can help with some of these questions, for instance class sizes and examination pass rates, but these do not form part of the financial accounts. However, they do affect the accounts. Small class sizes need more teachers, so more money has to be budgeted for and spent on employee costs. Despite this connection, the figure in the accounts for how much money is spent on employees does not directly translate into class sizes. So perhaps it would be reasonable to conclude that customers, in this case parents, are not making decisions based primarily on financial information about the business.

To sum up, financial stakeholders in a business are those people or organisations who have a financial interest in the business. This essentially means that they would be affected by the business doing financially better or worse. It is generally the case that the larger the business, the larger the number of financial stakeholders.

It is essential you are aware of the meaning of the key accounting terms introduced here before you proceed any further in this book. To consolidate your understanding, use your notes from Essential Reading 1, and the B120 Glossary if necessary, to make sure you feel confident about what the following key terms mean: *sole trader*, *partnership*, *unlimited liability*, *limited liability*, *private company*, *public company*. We will now use Activity 2.3 to help you to understand the difference between sole traders and public companies in terms of their stakeholders.

Activity 2.3

Spend about **15 minutes** on this activity

Purpose: to use another business example to compare the financial stakeholders involved in a small business such as that of a sole trader with the number of people involved in a large public company.

Task: for the two businesses described below, think about the possible financial stakeholders within the business (that is, internal) and outside the business (that is, external), and try to fill in the table:

1   Joleen Smith, a small UK based sole trader – she trades as 'Smith's Fruits' at a number of local outdoor markets, and has one employee, Sam Jones;

2   Tesco, a large UK-based public company.

Smith's Fruits		Tesco	
Internal financial stakeholders	External financial stakeholders	Internal financial stakeholders	External financial stakeholders

Feedback

The financial stakeholders that we suggest for each business are shown below. The main point to appreciate is that a large number of people are affected, for better or worse, by the financial well-being of a large public company such as Tesco.

Because financial stakeholders have an interest in the financial well-being of a business, they should also have an interest in the financial information it provides. Each financial stakeholder has a different perspective and thus a different interest in this financial information.

Smith's Fruits		Tesco	
Internal financial stakeholders	*External financial stakeholders*	*Internal financial stakeholders*	*External financial stakeholders*
Joleen Smith Sam Jones	One local bank if Joleen has an overdraft	Hundreds, possibly thousands of managers	Thousands of shareholders
	One or more suppliers of goods and services	Thousands of employees	Lenders of money
	Customers	Thousands of managers and employees who own shares in the company	Thousands of suppliers of goods and services
	HM Revenue and Customs		Thousands of customers and clients
	A limited number of competitors		A number of UK government agencies including HM Revenue and Customs
			Thousands of competitors
			The general public

It is very important that you appreciate the different types of financial information that different stakeholders need, and we have therefore included another activity on this topic to check your understanding.

Activity 2.4

Spend about 20 minutes on this activity

Purpose: to reflect further on the different types of financial information that different financial stakeholders require.

Task: to match different financial stakeholders with the financial information that they need. In the table below, the financial information in the second column is incorrectly associated with the stakeholders in the first column. Reflect on the financial information needs of the stakeholders and then choose the most appropriate financial information for each one.

Financial stakeholder	Financial information needed
Owner Has a vested interest in the business's future and success; tends to be financially conservative	• Evidence that a business will be able to pay the interest on any debts • The worth of a business should the debt be unpaid and the business forced to close
Investor/shareholder Invests money or has shares in a business; their analysis is often detailed and focused on short-term returns	• Reassurance that the business will continue to operate competitively • End-of-year figures that reflect their competence favourably
Lender Gives loans; needs to know that the interest is affordable and that the debt can be repaid	• How well the business is doing compared with previous years and with competitors • Reassurance that the source of income is safe and secure
Competitor Has an interest in the relative financial performance and business statistics of rivals	• Information on the business to allow comparisons with other businesses, with a view to choosing between them • Indications that financial returns will be maximised
Manager/employee Works for and is paid by the business on a full-time or regular basis	• Growth in sales, market share, net profits, and overall business efficiency • Information about the cost structure and operations of competitors
Customer/supplier Needs to know whether they are dealing with a financially sound and reputable business	• Properly prepared and computed accounts and profit and loss statements • Validity of accounts when compared with similar businesses
Taxation official Reviews financial statements for accuracy and reasonableness, then checks the amount of tax payable	• Continuity of supply and business without disruption to the flow of goods or services • Ability of the business to pay for goods and deliver on time

Feedback

After some reflection on the different information needs of the various stakeholders in a business, you should have been able to match the columns as indicated below.

Financial stakeholder	Financial information needed
Owner Has a vested interest in the business's future and success; tends to be financially conservative	• How well the business is doing compared with previous years and with competitors • Reassurance that the source of income is safe and secure
Investor/shareholder Invests money or has shares in a business; their analysis is often detailed and focused on short-term returns	• Information on the business to allow comparisons with other businesses, with a view to choosing between them • Indications that financial returns will be maximised
Lender Gives loans; needs to know that the interest is affordable and that the debt can be repaid	• Evidence that a business will be able to pay the interest on any debts • The worth of a business should the debt be unpaid and the business forced to close
Competitor Has an interest in the relative financial performance and business statistics of rivals	• Growth in sales, market share, net profits, and overall business efficiency • Information about the cost structure and operations of competitors
Manager/employee Works for and is paid by the business on a full-time or regular basis	• Reassurance that the business will continue to operate competitively • End-of-year figures that reflect their competence favourably
Customer/supplier Needs to know whether they are dealing with a financially sound and reputable business	• Continuity of supply and business without disruption to the flow of goods or services • Ability of the business to pay for goods and deliver on time
Taxation official Previews financial statements for accuracy and reasonableness, then checks the amount of tax payable	• Properly prepared and computed accounts and profit and loss statements • Validity of accounts when compared with similar businesses

2.4 The accounting equation and principles of double-entry bookkeeping

The system that accountants use to record financial data is known as ***double-entry bookkeeping***. Double-entry bookkeeping is based on the dual aspect rule, i.e. a recognition that every transaction has a twofold effect. For example, if I lend you £200, the transaction has a twofold effect on both of us:

- The effect on you: (1) your cash goes up by £200 and (2) what you owe me also goes up by £200.

- The effect on me: (1) my cash goes down by £200 and (2) what I am owed by you goes up by £200.

Financial transactions in the business world are usually recorded using some form of double-entry bookkeeping under which both aspects of every financial transaction are recognised. Much of the work of financial accountants consists of summarising financial information in accordance with generally accepted accounting principles. This information is derived from the double-entry bookkeeping system, which will be explained below. The system is based on the relationship between the key components of assets, expenses, liabilities, capital and income:

Assets: These are possessions or resources owned by a business. They include physical or tangible possessions such as property, plant, machinery, stock, and cash and bank balances. They also include intangible assets, i.e. non-physical possessions such as copyright and patent rights.

Expenses: The expenditure made by a business relating to the revenue generating activities, e.g. wages and salaries, property rental costs, the cost of goods bought or produced for resale.

Capital: This is the term used to describe the amount that the owners have invested in an entity. In effect, their 'capital' is the amount owed by the entity to its owners.

Liabilities: These are the opposite of assets. They are the amounts owed by a business to outside parties. They include loans, bank overdrafts, creditors, i.e. amounts owing to parties for the supply of goods and services to the business that have not yet been settled in cash.

Income: The money generated by the business by selling its goods or services.

There is an interdependent relationship between assets, expenses, capital, liabilities and income. It is frequently presented in the form of what is called the 'accounting equation':

$$\text{Assets} + \text{Expenses} = \text{Liabilities} + \text{Capital} + \text{Income}.$$

In other words, what the business has paid out in terms of possessions and expenses has been financed by a combination of funds provided by the owners and by creditors. As mentioned above, records of financial transactions of the vast majority of commercial organisations are made according to the double-entry bookkeeping system, which is based on the accounting equation. The system is highly structured and logical and enables even the largest businesses to keep track of their financial position over time.

As the name implies, double-entry bookkeeping requires each financial transaction to be recorded twice within the accounting records of the business, recognising the dual aspect of each transaction. For example, a business buying equipment with a cheque for £20,000 (1) receives £20,000 worth of equipment and (2) spends £20,000. In terms of the accounting equation we see that the increase in one asset (equipment + £20,000) is matched by the decrease in another asset (bank balance − £20,000). If the business sells goods for £5,000 to a customer paying by cheque, the business gives goods valued at £5,000 and receives a cheque for the same amount. The accounting equation stays in balance as the asset represented by the bank balance increases (+ £5,000) whilst income in the form of sales increases by the same amount.

Activity 2.5

Spend about **20 minutes** on this activity

Purpose: to reflect on your understanding of the accounting equation and the double-entry system.

Task: Look at the following transactions of John Daniel. How will they affect the accounting equation? Enter the changes to each component of the equation (as pluses and minuses) in the table below, and then show the overall effect on the accounting equation. The changes relating to the first two transactions have been entered as examples.

1 September Starts business by opening a bank account with £4,000

2 September Buys 2,000 items for resale with a cheque for £2,000

3 September Sells 500 items (which cost £1 each) for £700 cash

4 September Pays wages £300 by cash

5 September Buys stationery from Staples Ltd valued at £700. John expects to pay for the stationery in a month's time.

6 September Buys a computer with a cheque for £1,000.

7 September Sells 600 items (which cost £1 each) to Customer A for £820. Customer A intends to pay in two months' time.

8 September John pays £1,000 into the business bank account from his own savings.

9 September John draws out £100 from the business bank account for his own use.

10 September John buys 1,500 items for resale for £1,500 from Megabuys Ltd. and intends to pay for them in a month's time.

	Assets £	Expenses £		Liabilities £	Capital £	Income £
1	+4,000 (Bank)				+4,000	
2	−2,000 (Bank) +2,000 (Stock)					
3						
4						
5						
6						
7						
8						
9						
10						

Feedback

	Assets £	Expenses £		Liabilities £	Capital £	Income £
1	+4,000 (Bank)				+4,000	
2	−2,000 (Bank) +2,000 (Stock)					
3	−500 (Stock) +700 (Cash)	+500 (Cost of Sales)				+700 (Sales)
4	−300 (Cash)	+300 (Wages)				
5		+700 (Stationery)		+700 (Creditors)		
6	+1,000 (Computer) −1,000 (Bank)					
7	−600 (Stock) +820 (Debtor)	+600 (Cost of Sales)				+820 (Sales)
8	+1,000 (Bank)				+1,000	
9	−100 (Bank)				−100	
10	+1,500 (Stock)			+1,500 (Creditors)		

The overall effect of the ten transactions is:

Assets £	Expenses £		Liabilities £	Capital £	Income £
+6,520	+2,100		+2,200	+4,900	+1,520
	= + 8,620			= +8,620	

In transactions 1 and 8, John is increasing the value of his capital but transaction 9 reduces this value. When an owner takes out money or goods from the business, it is classed as 'drawings'.

In transactions 2 and 10, because the goods are for resale, they are regarded as 'stock'. Expenses such as stationery, petrol and so on, which are used up in running the business, are not classed as purchases of stock, but might be entered as 'office expenses', 'motor expenses' and so forth.

Transaction 3 and 7 are sales. Note that there are two things to consider – first, the reduction in levels of stock (at cost price) and then the recognition of the sale as income. This is how profit is recognised – first, by transferring the cost of goods sold to 'expenses', and then taking account of the sale as 'income'. You will note that there is a profit made in each of these two transactions.

In transaction 5, the stationery company is a creditor (a liability) until John pays the amount owing.

In transaction 6, the computer is a fixed asset, not an expense, as it is expected to last for several years and is of substantial value.

In transaction 7, Customer A is John's debtor (an asset of John) until she pays the amount owed.

The dual aspect of each financial transaction of a business is therefore recorded by the business in its double-entry bookkeeping system. Just as every transaction results in two adjustments being made to the accounting equation, two changes are also made to the accounting records. A change to the accounting records is called an *entry* and so we talk about making entries in the accounts. An *account* is simply a collection of entries relating to a particular type of transaction. The total amount of money recorded in an account is called the *balance* of that account. Accounts used to be kept in various bound books referred to as a ledger and all the **ledgers** used in a particular accounting system are known collectively as the *books of account*. Even though bookkeeping systems are usually computerised these days, it is still convenient to use these historical terms to describe aspects of modern accounting systems.

You may come across two special terms that bookkeepers have historically used to describe entries made in the books of account:

	Means an accounting entry that:	
Debit	Increases the balance in an asset or expense account	Decreases the balance in a liability, capital or income account
Credit	Increases the balance in a liability, capital or income account	Decreases the balance in an asset or expense account

We should stress that we are not trying to turn you into a bookkeeper. You do, however, need to know something about how accounting information is recorded and compiled before it is presented to you as a business manager.

The double-entry bookkeeping system described above records the business's assets, expenses, liabilities, capital and income. From time to time, a business needs to summarise its financial position by comparing its income with its expenditure over a specific period, in a statement known as a *profit and loss account*, and by summarising its assets and its liabilities (and therefore its capital) at the end of that period in a statement known as a *balance sheet*. These two key financial summaries are accounting summaries – and must therefore comply with the key concepts introduced to you in Session 3. It could be argued that all a business needs to understand its financial position is a summary of its cash and bank accounts (Section 2.4) – *a cash flow statement* which is introduced in Section 3.7.

2.5 Cash accounting

In simple terms, cash accounting is what is done to work out the balance in the cash till or bank account of a business (*note* – generally, when we talk about 'cash', we include all bank account balances. 'Cash' payments or receipts can be made by cheque or bank transfer, for example – in business transactions, actual cash in the form of notes and coins is not often involved except for the smallest transactions). Essentially cash accounting involves a comparison between what has gone in and what has gone out over the period of time since the balance was last calculated. Activity 1.2 in study Session 1 did this for Sue's travel agency – but using forecast information rather than looking at what had happened in the past.

As an illustration we shall use the balance figure on your personal bank statement or on the receipt from an ATM (automatic teller machine) when you get some money out. This figure is what the bank recognises as being in your account on that day. However, you may know that there are other transactions on your account that have not registered yet. For instance, you have just been shopping using your credit card, you paid your electricity bill with a cheque yesterday, and you paid a cheque in from your brother two days ago. So you will be able to calculate the resulting balance on the account from these figures. (At least you would be able to if you kept a record or kept all the slips of paper involved. You might be surprised to discover how many accountants I know who don't balance their bank account in this way!) This agreement of the bank account balance and the other records you have is an example of reconciliation. If financial information is kept in more than one place or in different formats regular reconciliations are needed to ensure that the different sets of records remain in accord with one another.

Like a person, businesses also need to know what cash is available in their bank accounts so that they can pay suppliers and loan interest, repay loans and pay staff. There needs to be sufficient to cover the payments as they fall due, but ideally no more than sufficient. Excess cash could be invested elsewhere, either in an interest-paying account or within the business. Businesses use cash flow forecasts to predict when and how much money is coming in and when they will need more or less cash for business operations. This informs decisions about when and how much to borrow or invest, as we saw with the example of Sue's travel agency.

So cash accounting is very useful. But it does not fully describe the financial position of the business or person. The reason you want to know what is in your bank account may be because you are due to pay another bill, say for telephone calls. You have already made the calls and incurred the costs, but the bill has not arrived yet. Once it does, it will have to be paid, thus reducing the amount of 'available' money in your bank account. Alternatively, you may know you are due a refund on your tax for last year, and once this arrives it will increase the amount of money in your account. This sort of reasoning may seem obvious, but what you are doing by taking out bills and adding in due amounts is calculating how much you have, whether or not it is in or out of the bank account yet.

The calculation of the current financial position is the basis of what accountants call *accrual accounting*. We will return to this in more detail later. However, in essence accrual accounting means that income includes everything earned by the business for a particular period, whether it has yet been received in cash or not. It also means that expenses include everything incurred by the business during that period, whether it has yet been paid or not. Some businesses use only cash accounting. Small cash-based businesses and new businesses often do not need, or cannot get, credit facilities, and do not extend them to their customers. Small charities (for instance in Scotland those with an annual turnover of up to £25,000) can choose to use cash accounting to make legally required reports. However, it is more normal for businesses in any sector to use accrual accounting for reporting to stakeholders, including any owners. Let's look in more detail at the cash account using the simple example below and Activity 2.5.

Example 2.1

Mr and Mrs Myers tell us about the flow of cash through their joint bank account over the last year.

'During this last year', says Mrs Myers, 'we had combined after-tax earnings of £31,000. The mortgage payments on the house were £8,400. It is a repayment mortgage and the payments cover interest of £5,950 and a repayment of £2,450 of the initial debt. Our council tax came to £950. Our rail fares were £1,600. The car cost £2,300 to run, including tax and insurance. Heating and lighting came to £850, and we spent £1,800 on a holiday. We spent £6,000 on food. The house insurance cost £600, and we paid £500 in life insurance premiums. All our other expenses came to £4,800. We began the year with £1,000 in our joint bank account.'

Activity 2.6

Spend about **30 minutes** on this activity

Purpose: to construct and interpret a simple cash account in a spreadsheet.

Task:

1   From the B120 course website under Book 3, download the Excel spreadsheet 'B120 Book 3 Cash Account'. This is included in the 30 minutes you should spend on this activity.

2   Using the cash flow information about Mr and Mrs Myers in Example 2.1 above, replace the zeros in the spreadsheet with the correct figures. (Ensure that you replace only the zeros you need as three zeros represent subtotals and totals, and contain formulae which need to remain.)

3   Change the figure for heating and lighting from £850 to £870.

   (a) How does this change the closing balance in the cash account?

   (b) What feature of a spreadsheet does this highlight?

4   Mr and Mrs Myers do a cash account once a year. What are the advantages of doing cash accounts more regularly?

Feedback

If you are new to downloading files as well as new to using Excel you will have done well to complete this activity.

1   Please contact the IT helpdesk if you have had any trouble downloading the Excel spreadsheet 'B120 Book 3 Cash Account' from the B120 website. See the B120 Study Companion for advice on how to do this.

2   The table below gives the correct figures.

Cash account for Mr and Mrs Myers for the last calendar year

	£	£
Cash inflow		
After tax earnings		31,000
Cash outflows		
Mortgage payments	8,400	
Council tax	950	
Rail fares	1,600	
Car running costs	2,300	
Heating and lighting	850	
Holiday expenses	1,800	
Food expenses	6,000	
House insurance	600	
Life insurance premiums	500	
Other expenses	4,800	
Total		27,800
Net inflow of cash during the year		3,200
Opening balance in the bank		1,000
Closing balance in the bank		4,200

3   (i) The closing balance would fall to £4,180.

(ii) This shows that changing one number in a spreadsheet also changes all other numbers that are linked to the first number by formulae. In this spreadsheet, three numbers, including the closing balance figure, are automatically changed. This is much easier than having to recalculate the figures by hand.

4   A more regular cash account, monthly for instance, would   help Mr and Mrs Myers to act more swiftly in response to changes to their cash balance. This might help them to avoid a short-term overdraft for instance, or allow them to transfer surplus cash to a savings or internet account that offers a higher interest rate. The same applies to the example of Sue's travel agency in Activity 1.2 in study Session 1.

We hope you have found the activities in this study session helpful in terms of reinforcing your understanding of some key accounting terms and concepts.

2.6 Conclusion

In this study session we introduced some key accounting terms and explained what differentiates types of entities, such as sole traders and companies, in the context of accounting. We also introduced a central feature of accounting in many, particularly small, businesses – cash accounting –

and used a simple online example to clarify its basic principles. In the next study session we explore the different types of accounting statements.

2.7 Learning outcomes

By the end of this study session on businesses and cash accounting you should be able to:

- differentiate between different types of business organisation and their accounting needs;
- describe the different types of financial stakeholders and explain why they need accounting information;
- explain what is meant by the 'accounting equation';
- understand the fundamental concept on which accounting is based;
- explain the basic principles of a cash account and of cash accounting.

You will have developed your learning by:

- completing and making notes on an essential reading about different types of businesses;
- downloading and manipulating a simple spreadsheet of a cash account example (Activity 2.5).

Session 3 The accounting statements

Why are we studying 'the accounting statements' prepared and used by businesses? The transactions that take place over a period of time can be summarised and analysed to provide information about what a business has done during that time. There are three accounting statements that are generally used to display this information. These are the profit and loss account, the balance sheet and the cash flow statement. You need to understand the contribution of these accounting statements to a business, what they reveal about the business and how they are used in running a business.

The **aims and objectives** of Session 3 are to:

* explain the use and relevance of the major accounting statements used by businesses – the profit and loss account, the balance sheet and the cash flow statement;

* highlight and define the key terms used in the context of these accounting statements.

'A financial statement that makes sense? Why would you want to see something boring like that?'

3.1 The three main accounting statements

* The three accounting statements that are generally used (and which are legally required to be produced by many companies and most public sector and charitable bodies as part of their annual reports) are:

* the ***profit and loss account*** (also known as the ***income statement***, the profit statement, the statement of financial performance, or the income and expenditure account);

* the ***balance sheet*** (also known as the statement of financial position);

* the ***cash flow statement***.

In this session, you are introduced to the financial statements produced by a small business. We trace the growth of a small company – Paula's Pipes.

Numerous accounting problems are encountered on the way. The owner is not an accountant but has to learn to understand and use financial accounts in order to successfully manage her company. You are presented with the problems as seen through the eyes of the owner of the company and by tackling the accounting statements to discover, as she does, the accounting knowledge required of the non-accountant.

3.2 The profit and loss account

The profit and loss account reports on certain financial aspects of transactions that have taken place during an accounting period. It does this by showing the income which has been earned and the expenses incurred in earning it. The difference between the two is a profit if the income is higher than the expenses or a loss if the expenses are higher than the income.

You will find that accounting and finance are no more immune to fashion than any other aspect of life, and in different countries and at different times the basic accounting statements have or have had different titles. You will also find that as your knowledge grows, you will recognise the individual accounting statements no matter what they are called.

Let us go back to Paula's Pipes, the small business example that was introduced in the last study session. We have created a fictional set of accounting statements to illustrate the points we want to make, with a set of notes afterwards to explain what each line of these accounts is about. We will start by looking at the profit and loss account. The capital letters in the left hand column are cross-referenced to the notes that follow the statement.

	A Paula's Pipes Profit and Loss Account for the period from 1 January to 31 December 2008	£	£
B	**Income**		**872,000**
C	Less cost of goods sold		
D	Opening stock	54,300	
E	Purchases	571,000	
		625,300	
F	Less closing stock	63,900	561,400
G	**Gross profit**		**310,600**
H	Less expenses:		
I	Transport expenses	2,000	
J	Rent	30,000	
	Rates	26,500	
	Insurance	7,800	
K	Wages and salaries	97,340	
L	Marketing expenses	2,160	
M	Administration expenses	23,000	
N	Interest on long-term loan	2,000	
O	Depreciation	73,000	263,800
P	**Net profit**		**46,800**

(A) As this is a profit and loss account it has a title that indicates the period of time that is being covered.

(B) 'Income' could also be called 'Sales', 'Revenue' or 'Turnover'. Income is the total amount of sales invoiced in the period. Several different types of income could be shown here if Paula wanted to monitor them, for instance splitting her work between repairs and new installations, or water supplies and drains. There could also be income from ancillary activities, such as selling plumbing components from her stock, or renting part of her store room to a joiner. The important point here is to show the information in a way that is useful to Paula.

However this is done, the profit and loss account will be prepared using accrual accounting. As we mentioned briefly in study Session 2, this means that the income shown here is the income actually earned in the period covered by the statement. If Paula gives her customers credit (instead of asking for payment immediately a job is completed) then she will probably have some uncollected fees at the end of each accounting period. The implication of accrual accounting for the figure of income earned for the period is that all amounts billed will be included, even if some of the cash has not yet been collected from her customers. We will discuss this further in Sections 3.3 and 3.4.

(C) The sales are made of specific goods and the cost of these specific goods is matched against the sales to determine the gross profit. The idea is that each sale generates a profit which equals the sale price less the cost of whatever was sold. The total gross profit for the year is the total of such profits. This cost in not usually measured directly but is implied by the calculation (D) and (F).

(D) Firstly the **stock** of goods for sale at the beginning of the period at 1 January 2008 is considered. This total will have been arrived at by counting the goods and valuing them at cost. (This can be modified but is a complication we will ignore for the moment).

(E) Then the total amount of goods for resale purchased in the year is added. All such goods purchased in the year are included irrespective of the date of payment. This gives the total of goods in stock at the beginning and of goods added to stock in the year (£625,300). This is the total cost of goods which could have been sold in the year.

(F) However, not all such goods were sold and the unsold ones are counted and valued at input cost and deducted from the goods that could have been sold to give the cost of the goods that actually were sold in the year.

(G) '**Gross profit**' is a heading used in the profit and loss account to show the profit from activities (sales less costs directly related to those sales) before the remainder of the costs of running the business are deducted. From Paula's point of view it is the amount available to meet all these other costs and to reward her for her work.

The figure of gross profit is considered useful by many businesses because it helps them evaluate the success of their main trading strategy before considering the effect of other expenses that have been incurred.

(H) The term '**Expenses**' covers the indirect costs of producing this period's income. Different sectors use different categories, and there are rules for statements that are legally required to be prepared for external users.

However, for small businesses like Paula's Pipes or for internal use the expenses can be analysed in whatever way is most useful to the owners and managers of the business.

(I) 'Transport expenses' is a standard heading in many sets of accounts. All the running costs of the van go under this heading.

(J) Rent, rates and insurance are common expenses. For example, the rent for the year will be in accordance with the lease and the amount included reflects amounts *incurred* for the period not just the amounts *paid* in the period.

(K) 'Wages and salaries' include the wages and salary cost of employing staff in the year. It is usually calculated as gross remuneration payable plus employer's taxes and pension contributions.

(L) 'Marketing expenses' are often separated out. In this case Paula wanted to know how much she had spent on advertising in proportion to the rest of her costs and income.

(M) The category 'Administration expenses' is often used for the costs of running an office – stationery and telephone costs might go here, for example. Once again, it is really up to the owners and managers of small businesses how they ask their accountants to categorise the various expenses.

(N) Paula pays 10% interest on a long-term loan she took out to help buy plant and equipment. The interest is shown here as an expense in the profit and loss account, although in larger businesses such interest costs are shown separately as 'financing costs'.

(O) *Depreciation* on fixed assets is related to the concept of capital expenditure. Capital expenditure means the acquisition of fixed assets. Fixed assets are things (e.g., plant, machinery, vehicles etc.) which last a long time and cost more than a trivial amount. For example, buying a new machine for £10,000 in the year ending 31 January 2009 does not reduce the profit for that year by £10,000 but does reduce the profit for the whole five years for which it is expected to be in use. Thus there is a reduction of profit in the year:

$$\frac{£10,000}{5} = £2,000$$

which is known as depreciation. Note that there is an element of judgement in assessing the depreciation cost – how long will an asset last? What will be its value at the end of that period? The answers to these questions will form the basis of what accountants call a 'depreciation policy', which we will look at in Section 3.4 below.

(P) The final figure, the *net profit*, shows what is left of the income after all the costs related to it have been allowed for. If the costs were greater than the income then there would be a loss rather than a profit.

There are several points that may have occurred to you when looking at this simplified profit and loss account. For instance:

- Why does income cover only work completed in the period rather than work actually done in the period? What about jobs that are still being worked on?

- The original purchase cost of the van does not seem to appear under the heading 'Transport costs'. Why not?

- Tax is not shown here as a cost. Why?

- What about Paula? There has been no mention of what she is taking out of the business for herself.

These questions are addressed in the next three sections.

Before moving on to Section 3.3, however, we would like you to do a short activity. We have explained the idea of gross profit as the difference between sales income and costs directly related to those sales. All other expenses (described as indirect expenses) were shown separately after the gross profit was calculated.

Activity 3.1

Spend about **15 minutes** on this activity

Purpose: to consider the usefulness of the distinction made by accountants between direct and indirect costs.

Task: imagine you own and run a small neighbourhood grocery shop. Consider the following questions:

1 What type of items do you think your direct costs would cover?

2 What do you think would come under the heading of 'Expenses' and would therefore be your indirect costs?

3 Why do you think this distinction might be useful to you in managing the business?

Feedback

1   As your main activity in trading is to sell goods, the cost to you of the groceries you sell in the shop is directly related to your level of sales. The more you sell, the more you spend on the groceries that are sold. Unless you offer quantity discounts, in principle if you double your sales in a week the cost to you of the goods you sell will be roughly double. You may have put staff costs here, but this would be reasonable only if you hire your staff by the hour and can adjust their working times depending on how busy you are.

2   Your indirect costs are many and varied. You probably put down items like the rent of the shop premises, heating and lighting, telephone, any local authority taxes such as business rates (in the UK) and staff (but see the previous paragraph).

3   The key to why this distinction might be useful to you in managing the business lies in how the different types of costs may be affected by changes in sales revenue. Suppose that you believe you can sell 50 per cent more goods in your shop. In theory this means that your gross profit should rise by 50 per cent too, so having this figure will help with your planning. However, you also need to look closely at your indirect costs. Some of these will not change if you sell 50 per cent more; for example your rent is unlikely to change. However, you will probably find that your telephone bill rises slightly as you order more goods. You may need to open longer hours to achieve this higher level of sales, so your heating and lighting costs will rise, and you will need to hire more staff or pay overtime. Nevertheless, these costs will not rise exactly in proportion to the rise in sales income.

3.3 Recognising revenues

The basis of accrual accounting is that each period's accounts show the financial effects of what has happened to the business during that period. The problem is that real life events do not usually happen in discrete parts. Whilst accounting may divide time into convenient periods, it is unlikely that the ends of the periods will coincide with any natural breaks in business. So, although businesses try to choose period-ends that fall during quiet periods, there will still be a continuation in activities from one year or period into the next. Many businesses are not particularly seasonal. For example, Paula's Pipes has extra summer work from new installations and winter work from burst pipes, which evens out over the year.

Other businesses have much longer cycles: pastoral agriculture and forestry, for instance. If trees take sixty years to grow to a saleable size, does that mean that the forester's accounts show nothing for income for sixty years? That would certainly be the case if cash accounting were used because until the trees are sold there is no money coming in. Under accrual accounting, on the other hand, an estimate can be made of the increase in value during the year. A valuation of the timber is made at the beginning and end of the year and the difference between the two valuations can be counted as income.

Different industries have different problems in deciding what to count as income. This issue of recognising revenues is now addressed by accounting regulations: they have particular rules, or standards, for certain businesses such as agriculture, forestry and construction, all of which may have longer production cycles than accounting cycles.

Let's take a closer look at accrual accounting and Paula's Pipes. Suppose that in November Paula takes on a large job plumbing a new clinic, expecting it to run until February. If she is counting only the revenue from completed jobs as income then, when Paula prepares her accounts to December, she is ignoring work done during November and December. Her accounts for the following February will however include the income from all four months of the clinic job, even though half of it was earned during the previous accounting year.

Activity 3.2

Spend up to about **10 minutes** on this activity

Purpose: to consider the implications of accounting for income for a specific job in Paula's Pipes.

Task: reflect on the following questions.

1   What might be the effects of accounting for the income from the clinic job in the way described above?

2   What difference would it make if the clinic job took only one day a week, and the rest of the week was used for smaller, quicker jobs?

Feedback

1   Accounting for the clinic job revenue entirely when it is finished in February would distort the picture shown by the accounts: the periods November to January would look less busy than they really were, and the period of February correspondingly busier. Also, if the costs of components used in the clinic job are included in the accounts as the components are used, then the November, December and January accounts include component costs that should be matched with the revenues recorded in the February accounts. This second breach of accrual principles makes the picture even less clear, with profit even more depressed in the first period and more enhanced in the second.

Comparisons between periods will therefore be confused. To avoid this confusion, larger businesses estimate the value of work that has been done but not yet billed for, and instead of counting income from work *completed* in the period they count income from work *done* in the period. As the clinic job is an unusually long job for this business, Paula should probably make an adjustment to her figures to put some of the profit back into November, December and January. Of course, she would also need to make equivalent reductions in February.

There are other issues here that Paula (or her accountant) ought to consider before deciding how to deal with these adjustments. If she adjusts her figures as suggested above, this will increase her profit for the period November to January and reduce it for February. This may reflect more fairly what she has actually earned, but it may also mean (because she will be preparing annual accounts for the year to December) that she pays some tax earlier than she would otherwise have done. Tax is complicated so we will not go into this in any detail, but it is something to bear in mind.

2   If the clinic job were providing only one-fifth of the workload then the distortion of the accounts between periods would be much less. In this situation it might not be worthwhile adjusting the figures. This is an example of the materiality principle (as described in Section 1.2) in operation.

3.4 Recognising expenses

Although Paula's van cost £5,300, the purchase cost does not show in the profit and loss account as an expense. This is because vans normally last longer than a single accounting period. Remember that the profit and loss account shows what income has been earned in the period and what expenses were incurred in earning it. To include all the cost of the van would be an overstatement, yet as the van has been used during the year some of the cost should surely be in the accounts as an expense. Accountancy deals with this problem by the use of depreciation. Depreciation divides the cost of long-lasting purchases into smaller amounts that are then charged as expenses over the number of years that the purchase is expected to last.

Activity 3.3

Spend about **5 minutes** on this activity

Purpose: to understand how costs are shown differently in accounting statements based on our on-going, small business example – Paula's Pipes.

Task: consider the following based on your understanding of the previous sections. Both Paula's van and the insurance premium for it last for more than one financial period. What are the differences in the way that their costs are reflected in the profit and loss account?

Feedback

There are a lot of similarities and only one real difference. Both costs can be divided into amounts to be charged as expenses in successive periods. The difference is that Paula knows the van's insurance will run for a year, but can only guess or estimate how long she will use the van for and what its ultimate trade-in value will be.

The purpose of the profit and loss account is to show the income that was earned in the period and the expenses which were incurred in order to achieve that income. (This is accrual accounting, which we discussed earlier in this session.) Therefore, to deal with situations like this, accountants make adjustments for expenses that fall into more than one financial period. These adjustments bring the expenses recorded in the profit and loss account into line with the benefit that has been provided in the accounting period under consideration.

In the case of the insurance premium that Paula has paid for the van, only the proportion of the expense that falls into the current period will be shown in the profit and loss account. The amount that relates to the next accounting period (known as a **prepayment**) will be carried forward and shown in the profit and loss account for that period.

There may also be the opposite problem: some of the expenses of Paula's business may be billed in arrears (for example, telephone bills) and she may not receive these bills until after the end of the accounting period. In these cases it will be necessary to make an estimate of the amounts due so that the expense can be included in Paula's accounting statements. It will not be difficult to do this, because by the time the accounting statements are being prepared the bill will probably have arrived. Somewhat confusingly, this type of adjustment is called 'making an accrual'.

As we discussed earlier, depreciation is accountants' way of recognising the fact that long-lasting purchases will give benefit to the business for more than one accounting period. As noted above, there is a difference between depreciation and other business expenses, because depreciation has to be based on estimates. Paula (or her accountant) will have to think about how long she is likely to use the van before deciding that she needs to replace it, and how much it might be worth at that time – which may be several years in the future.

Finally, as we saw in Section 3.2, only those components actually used by Paula in earning her income for the current accounting period should be shown as an expense. Any components not used at the end of the accounting period will be carried forward to be used in the next accounting period. At the end of the current accounting period Paula will need to make an estimate of the value of the unused components – her stock or **inventory**.

These adjustments may sound complicated, but in fact they are relatively straightforward and routine for accountants to deal with. We summarise below the points you need to remember from this discussion and consider further some of the issues raised.

- The profit and loss account is prepared using accrual accounting, which differs from cash accounting. What is important in this method is not when cash comes in or goes out, but when the business's income is earned, and when its expenses are incurred.

- For some very simple businesses cash accounting will be perfectly acceptable. These will be businesses where income is received in cash as it is earned (a street-corner newspaper seller perhaps), where expenses are paid for in cash when they are incurred (the newspaper seller again), and which do not make significant long-lasting purchases (maybe our newspaper seller once more).

- However, such businesses are comparatively rare. Most businesses, even small ones, will use accrual accounting. As we have seen, this will involve making estimates and judgements. This raises some interesting issues:

- Making estimates sounds like guesswork, and it is in many cases! It is here that accountants can fall back on the principle of materiality, which we discussed in Session 1. Under this principle we need not worry too much about relatively minor items that will not affect users' decision making. We just need to take care that there is not a cumulative effect: many small estimates may add up to quite a large overall total.

- Accountants make these estimates based on their professional judgement. However, these are still estimates and therefore they cannot be 'right' – they will be a matter of opinion. Therefore, it is also the case that a business's profit cannot be 'right' or 'wrong'. Different accountants will come up with slightly different, but equally acceptable, profit figures for the same business's results. Accountants have the image of being score-keepers, but accountancy is not like keeping track of the score in a sporting event such as cricket.

- A better way of thinking about profit as measured by the profit and loss account is that there will be a range of possible figures for a given situation. This is an inevitable result of making different estimates and judgements.

3.5 Taking money out

Paula's profit and loss account in Section 3.2 deducted all expenses due to third parties except the tax authorities. Also, it did not show any amounts paid to Paula by the business. These could have been included in the category of administration costs but we assume that there was nothing for Paula there. Both these facts seem odd: the tax authorities are undoubtedly interested in Paula's business and will wish to charge her tax on her profits; and Paula herself requires an income. Why else is she in business?

These two issues are linked. The key is the status of Paula's business. In study Session 2 we identified Paula's Pipes as an example of a sole trader. Paula is in business on her own, and her business is not a limited company. This means that, so far as the law is concerned, the affairs of Paula and her business are not separate. However, for accounting purposes Paula's accountant will prepare the business's accounting statements as though Paula and her business were two quite separate entities. So, for example, Paula's personal expenses – such as holiday expenses or other non-business costs – will not appear in the business's profit and loss account. This is useful for Paula and for other interested parties as it means that the profit and loss account shows how profitable her business is irrespective of what she has spent on personal items.

The tax authorities, however, are interested in taxing Paula herself, on her taxable income from all sources. Remember that the law makes no distinction between Paula and her business. Paula's annual tax return will therefore report any profits she makes from her business, and any taxable income she may have received from other sources – for example, she may have investments and thus receive interest or dividends. Therefore her final tax bill is composed of tax on all her sources of income, less any personal allowances that she is entitled to as an individual (businesses do not get personal allowances), and cannot really be broken down and allocated to the different sources of income. This is why her profit and loss account does not show any tax charged.

What about Paula herself? This is a rather more contentious issue. Paula is the owner/manager of her business. She works full time for it. So it would seem reasonable that she should make a charge for her time. Looking at it from another point of view, suppose that Paula fell ill and decided to keep her business going by hiring another plumber to work for her. She would then pay her new employee and charge the costs of their wages as a business expense. So what is different about paying herself a wage and charging that as a business expense? The difference is that it is her business and she could pay herself just what she liked. If her profits were good, she could pay herself an enormous salary and reduce her profits for tax purposes to a much lower level. This argument gets a bit tricky, because you could argue that she would pay tax on her enormous salary instead, and the remaining business profits could then be taxed. Despite this, over time it has become accepted practice (and it's probably the simplest solution to the problem) that even if owners of businesses work in their business, anything they take out of the business for themselves is not shown as a business expense. This is worth bearing in mind when evaluating how profitable a sole trader's business is. To get a fair picture of the profits when a business is sold, an allowance would normally be made for a reasonable return to the owner.

Back to Paula and her personal income. Of course she takes money out of her business for herself. It's just that this is not called wages or a salary, and it is not treated as a business expense. What Paula takes out of her business is up to her. Her accountant will work out how much she has taken out – most likely by asking her and going through the business's bank account – and call it her *drawings*. (This is probably a corruption of the word 'withdrawal'.) It will be shown separately in her accounting statements, along with what she put in to start her business off when she first began in business on her own. Just as she would have put in money when she first started, so she can take money out when she wishes. Note that partnerships are treated in the same way.

We now briefly consider the position of limited companies. The law treats limited companies as separate entities. Under UK company law, companies have what is called 'separate legal personality'. A practical way of thinking about this is that companies can sue and be sued in their own name. Therefore they pay their own tax. So you will see taxation in the accounting statements of companies, unlike the accounts of sole traders. The owners of limited companies are called the *shareholders*, and they usually expect a direct return from their investment in the form of *dividends*. For companies, dividends are the equivalent of Paula's drawings. They are not business expenses; they are what the owners of the business (the shareholders) are taking out for themselves.

3.6 The balance sheet

The balance sheet shows the financial position of a business at a point in time, as one accounting period ends and another starts. Accounting time could be described as a stream of profit and loss accounts punctuated at regular intervals by balance sheets. Each accounting period is bracketed by two balance sheets. By comparing them the person reading the balance sheet can find information about the state of the business at the end of the period covered by the profit and loss account.

There are five basic accounting elements. Two of these – income and expenses – appear in the profit and loss account, as we have seen. The other three – *assets*, *liabilities* and *equity* – appear on the balance sheet. In the following sections we examine each of these and then give an example of a balance sheet.

Assets

In financial terms assets are things owned or controlled by the business that can generate future benefits in the form of income or services. These things can be of any size and may be tangible or intangible. Tangible assets are literally those things owned or controlled by a business that can be touched – an example might be motor vehicles. Intangible assets, on the other hand, cannot be touched – an example might be money invested in another business. If something cannot be owned or controlled by the business, then even if it will probably generate future income it cannot be counted as an asset of that business. Activity 3.4 below will help you to understand what can and cannot be owned or controlled.

Activity 3.4

Spend about **15 minutes** on this activity

Purpose: to understand what assets are.

Task: for each of the items below consider if they can be owned or controlled by a business, what sort of future benefit, income or services they might bring and if you think they qualify as assets:

Item	Owned/ controlled?	Future benefit	Asset or not?
An office building			
A set of screwdrivers			
Cash in a bank account			
Excellent relations with customers			
A patent			
A talented designer			
A store of food			
Unexpired insurance cover			
A debt owed to the business			

Feedback

An office building can be owned or controlled through a long lease or via ownership of the freehold, and will provide benefits in the form of accommodation for the business, or income if it is let to other users or sold. It will qualify as an asset.

A set of screwdrivers can be owned and could be used to adjust or construct something of benefit to the business, so should qualify as an asset. However, screwdrivers may be treated as expenses even though they will last more than one accounting period, because their value may be insignificant to the business.

Cash in a business's bank account qualifies as an asset because it is owned by the business and can be used in future to pay for expenses, which in turn bring benefits such as income to the business or the provision of services to the public.

Excellent relations with customers might bring future benefits to the business, but are unlikely to be something that can be controlled or owned, so cannot qualify as an asset.

A patent can be owned or controlled. For example, medicine patents are commonly licensed to drugs manufacturers by larger drugs companies. A patent can also bring future benefits by preventing competitors from producing patented items. Like other intellectual assets, patents are examples of intangible assets.

A talented designer should bring future benefits to the business, but can he or she be owned or controlled? This question applies to all employees. Performance contracts with artistic performers or sportspeople can count as assets as they preclude the person performing for someone else without the permission of the contract holder; this indicates a degree of control. The expression 'our people are our most important assets' may be more than just rhetoric for a business that values its staff, but it does not often mean that they are assets that could appear on a balance sheet. The practice of insuring show business and sports stars, as noted in Example 3.1 below, is an indication of how some people are regarded as assets.

A store of food could bring future benefits and can be owned. So, assuming the expiry dates are some time in the future, it would count as an asset, as do most stores of goods.

When a business pays an insurance premium it then owns that insurance cover. This could bring future benefits if there is a claim on the insurance and in any case it provides legally required cover, for instance public liability insurance, or peace of mind, both of which can be seen as benefits. When looking at prepayments in Section 3.4 we saw that insurance premiums can be allocated to different accounting periods. The 'used' part of the premium counts as an expense in the period to which it applies. The unexpired insurance cover is the part that applies to the next period after the balance sheet date. During that following period the asset called 'unexpired insurance cover' or 'prepaid insurance premium' is used up and so becomes an expense.

Debts owed to the business should lead to payment, which is an inflow of cash and therefore a benefit to the business. Debts are initially owned by the business that is owed the money, but can be sold on to organisations called debt factors that will attempt to collect the debts. Debts thus normally count as assets. Note that debts can collectively be called 'debtors' or 'accounts receivable'.

The following example illustrates some unusual types of assets.

Example 3.1

England striker Michael Owen is the latest in a long line of stars who have felt it necessary to insure the assets that made them famous.

The £60m valuation Liverpool have put on Owen is the highest known for a footballer and reflects the 18-year-old's soaring worth since his impressive displays in France [World Cup 1998].

...

Hollywood stars, pop stars and entire sports teams are now insured for millions of pounds.

The trend was begun by Hollywood star Betty Grable who insured her famous legs for $1m in the 1940s.

Gene Kelly, Mae West, Frank Sinatra and Sir Laurence Olivier were among the scores of legendary film stars who followed suit and have been insured by Lloyds of London.

Also on the books of the world famous underwriters have been The Beatles, Michael Jackson, The Rolling Stones and Duran Duran.

Lord of the Dance star Michael Flatley has had his legs insured for £25m, Ken Dodd's trademark teeth are insured for £4m while supermodels Naomi Campbell, Claudia Schiffer and Christie Turlington have cover totalling millions.

...

In December last year catwalk models refused to don the latest six inch heels at the Clothes Show Live exhibition without being insured.

They only paraded along the catwalk after their legs had been insured for £50,000.

Suzanne Moore, of the Association of British Insurers, says: 'The figure being quoted in connection with Michael Owen refers to his transfer value.

Players stand to make a lot of money over a fairly short career so if they're injured they will also lose money.'

(Source: BBC, 1998)

Liabilities

Liabilities can be seen as the opposite to assets: they will cause an outflow of benefits in the form of costs or commitments in the future. They are usually debts of the business that are, or will become, legally payable to other entities known as **creditors**. Paula's Pipes has various sources of liabilities: unpaid bills for components from the plumbers' merchant, the bank loan for a new van Paula has decided to buy, and deposits from customers for work that has not yet been done. Paula is liable to pay the supplier and tax collector and liable to do the work she has already been paid for.

Liabilities are usually more straightforward for a business to measure than are many assets, because they are normally payments due to other entities and will therefore be referred to in money terms.

Equity

The balance sheet shows the assets and the liabilities of the business by summarising and listing them at their monetary values. The difference between them is known as equity. This figure can be thought of as the amount the owner(s) have invested in the business. Suppose that a business decided to close down. All the assets would be sold (or 'realised' as accountants often put it) and all liabilities would have to be settled. What then remained in the business's bank account would belong to the owner(s) of the business. So the difference between assets and liabilities – the equity – is the stake of the owner(s) of the business.

You may think of some problems with this. What if, for example, the total of assets is worth less than the total of liabilities? This does happen. When it does, it means that the business cannot pay all its liabilities and in some circumstances the owner(s) may have to make a contribution. You may recall from Essential Reading 1 in study Session 2 that the shareholders of limited companies are protected in such a situation as the company is responsible for its own debts. However, for now, focus on the basic situation just described, which can be shown as a simple model that arises from the accounting equation (see Session 2.4 above):

$$\text{Assets} + \text{Expenses} = \text{Liabilities} + \text{Capital} + \text{Income}$$

This can be re-arranged as follows:

$$\text{Assets} - \text{Liabilities} = \text{Capital} + \text{Income} - \text{Expenses}$$

And, as you have seen above, 'Income – Expenses' = 'Profit'. So the value of the business to the owner – its 'Equity' – is the total of the capital invested plus any profit earned. And that leaves us with the final model that is the basis of the Balance Sheet:

$$\text{Assets} - \text{Liabilities} = \text{Equity}$$

You may have sometimes wondered why Balance Sheets balance. The reason is that they represent the sum total of all accounting entries made that, under the double entry system, satisfy the accounting equation as represented by this model. Changes in equity reflect the underlying changes in the assets and liabilities of the business.

Some of the other names used for equity are:

- capital
- net worth
- owner's interest in the business
- accumulated funds
- shareholders' funds
- shareholders' equity

These do not all mean precisely the same thing, because different terminology is used depending on the type of business and how it is constituted. At this stage, however, you just need to be able to identify this part of the balance sheet and what it represents.

Let us now look at the balance sheet at Paula's Pipes to make sure of our understanding of assets, liabilities and equity.

A	**Paula's Pipes Balance Sheet at 31 December 2008**			
B	Fixed assets/Long-term assets	£	£	£
C		Cost	Depreciation	Net book value
D	Plant and equipment	98,000	56,000	42,000
	Vehicles	41,000	17,000	24,000
E		139,000	73,000	66,000
F	**Current assets/Short-term assets**			
G	Stock/inventory		63,900	
H	Debtors/trade receivables		164,200	
I	Prepayments		1,800	
J			229,900	
K	**Current liabilities/Short-term liabilities**			
L	Creditors/trade payables		95,400	
M	Banks overdrafts		102,700	
N			198,100	
O	**Net current assets/Working capital**			31,800
P	**Total assets less current liabilities**			97,800
Q	**Long-term liabilities**			
	Loan at 10%			20,000
R				**77,800**
S	**Capital/Equity**			
T	As at 1 January 2008			68,100
U	Net profit for the year			46,800
V				114,900
W	Less drawings			37,100
X	As at 31 December 2008			**77,800**

(A) As this is a balance sheet it has a title that shows a point in time rather than a period of time.

(B) There are several categories of fixed assets, or long-term assets as they are often known (land, buildings, plant, vehicles, office equipment, etc.). The theory is that all fixed assets except land have limited lives because they wear out, or become obsolete. Consequently, fixed assets (except for land) need to be depreciated. Even buildings, for example, have limited (if extended) useful lives and therefore are depreciated. Commonly the useful life is estimated at 40 to 50 years. Plant and vehicles have shorter lives (5 to 10 years) and will be depreciated accordingly.

(C) It is usual to show three figures for each category of fixed assets:

- the original cost to the business
- the total amount by which the asset has depreciated since its acquisition
- the difference, which is called the net book value or written down value.

This value is derived from the original cost of the asset and will probably bear no resemblance at all to the possible amount for which the asset might be sold. This usually surprises people new to accounting.

(D) Two categories of fixed assets are included here. Sometimes there are more such as land and buildings (see under B above).

(E) Totals are given. We can see the total 'value' of the fixed assets.

(F) Current assets (short-term assets) are assets that comprise cash or which, through trading activities, will result in cash at some stage in the near future.

(G) Stock is as counted at 31 December 2008 and valued at cost, not selling price. Some items may be valued at less than cost. You will note that this item also appears in the profit and loss account. Calculation of stock quantity and value is time consuming and the problem of stock determination is one reason why financial statements are not produced more frequently than annually (although many businesses do produce monthly or quarterly or half yearly accounts).

(H) Some businesses sell goods and receive payment at the same time. When you buy groceries at the supermarket you might pay cash at the check out. However many businesses sell goods on credit. This means that on a sale, the sale is evidenced by the sending of an invoice to the customer setting out the goods sold and the amount due. Most invoices also state that payment is due at some specific time. Often this is 30 days after the sale. In practice customers often ignore this and pay rather later. This whole business of credit is a major problem to many companies. Since Paula sells on credit there will always be some customers who have had goods and not yet paid for them. These customers are called ***debtors*** and at each year end the total amount of sales invoiced for which payment has not been received will be assessed and included in the assets as debtors.

(I) When expenses such as fire insurance or rent are paid the payment is often for a period in advance. For example, for fire insurance for the calendar year 2008, £600 may be paid on 1 December that year. This means that at the year end at 31 December, 11 months' fire insurance cover has been paid for and is still to be enjoyed. This is $11/12 \times £600 = £550$ and would be included in the assets as a prepayment.

(J) The total of the current assets is shown. There can be other categories of current assets. A great number of businesses will have cash in the bank. Manufacturing business will have work in progress. Some will have various kinds of short-term investments such as bank deposits.

(K) Liabilities are usually shown in two separate sections. Current liabilities (short-term liabilities) which are those for which payment is due soon after the year end (in fact up to one year after the year end) and long-term liabilities which are those such as loans which will be settled more than one year after the year end. Not all businesses have long-term liabilities.

(L) Just as Paula offers credit to her customers so she takes credit from her suppliers. At the balance sheet date it is necessary to count up the amount she owes for goods and services which she has received but for which payment has not been made.

(M) Many businesses borrow money from their bankers on overdraft. In fact the principal source of income to the high street banks is interest charged to business customers and the principal source of money to business is the bank loan or overdraft. Overdrafts are forms of borrowing in which the amount borrowed changes continually as money is paid in and cheques are drawn. For most businesses an overdraft once taken out is constantly renewed and is a form of long-term liability. However as it is technically repayable on demand, an overdraft is normally included among the short-term liabilities.

(N) The total of short-term liabilities is shown. Note that in the past short-term liabilities were always called current liabilities but you might also see the modern term in balance sheets: 'creditors: amounts falling due within one year'.

(O) A single figure for current assets less the short-term liabilities is normally shown. This total is sometimes called the working capital. Working capital can be defined simply as current assets less current liabilities. Managers and accountants often speak of having a working capital problem. Essentially what they mean by this is an inability to pay creditors when they want to, as the overdraft has a limit which cannot be exceeded. The reason why working capital comes into this problem can be explained. For example, most firms find that stock has a tendency to increase even without an increase in business sales and that customers have a tendency to take longer to pay for goods supplied to them. When customers do not pay on time, money becomes tight and the firm tends to take longer before paying suppliers. Paying suppliers on time when customers do not pay on time may require an increase in overdraft and, unless this is agreed by the bank, trouble may ensue.

(P) The total assets less current liabilities is shown.

(Q) Liabilities such as mortgages and loans which have a repayment requirement more than one year away are included here. Paula has only one such liability which is a loan. Usually the interest rate is shown. The 10% means that Paula must pay 10% of the sum outstanding (i.e. 10% × £20,000 = £2,000) every year as long as the £20,000 remains outstanding.

(R) The total assets less liabilities is then shown as a single figure of net assets. The net assets figure will equal the equity figure, due to the application of the accounting equation, as discussed above.

(S) Equity is the assets less liabilities of the business expressed as a total sum. Some people describe it as the net worth. Just as a person might add up his fortune by valuing his assets (house, car, money in building societies, etc. less his liabilities – mortgage, hire purchase commitment, unpaid gas bill, etc.) and thus find out how rich he is, so a business prepares a balance sheet.

This section shows the changes in equity over the period of time since the previous balance sheet was prepared. It shows the equity of Paula's Pipes at the start of the current accounting period, adds in any profits made (or deducts any losses), then subtracts any amounts withdrawn by the owner(s) of the business – in this case, by Paula. Basically, what it is showing is that Paula's business has grown because it has made a profit but that Paula has then taken out some of that profit for herself. Paula decides how much she withdraws, but the amount taken will affect the money left in the business for the future.

(T) This figure is the balance sheet value of the assets less liabilities in total at the beginning of the year.

(U) The net profit for the year adds to the total assets less liabilities.

(V) This sum is often included but does not have any real significance.

(W) The owner may withdraw cash and goods from the business at various times during the year and the total is shown here.

(X) If all accounting has been done accurately and correctly, this figure of the capital at the end of the year will be the same figure as the assets less liabilities.

You should have got the idea from the notes above that there is a lot of variation in the way that balance sheet information is presented. Not all balance sheets will be laid out in this way. Some list all assets and then all liabilities, so there is no calculation for working capital. Some show long-term assets plus short-term assets less short-term liabilities, and this figure is then equal to a funding section that consists of equity plus long-term liabilities. This last method purports to show the value of the business, and then how it has been funded – through loans and equity. Different businesses may want to highlight different aspects of their finances. There are rules that apply to companies and especially companies listed on a stock exchange about what has to be shown, but within these rules there are many choices. Different countries also have different rules and customs.

If you understand the three accounting elements that will be on the balance sheet – assets, liabilities and equity – you will be able to start to interpret any layout. Think of them, and their sub-components, that is, long- and short-term assets and liabilities, as the building blocks of the balance sheet. It might be a good idea at this point, or at the end of this study session, to visit the accounts pages on the websites of one or two businesses that you know so that you can see these variations in practice.

Activity 3.5

Spend about **10 minutes** on this activity

Purpose: to test your understanding of assets, liabilities and equity.

Task: categorise the items in the table below, and for assets and liabilities state whether they are long or short term. We have completed the first one for you.

Item	Asset	Liability	Equity	Type
Packing machine	✓			Long term
Office computer				
Mortgage on offices				
School building				
Copyright for a song				
Pay owed to employee at balance sheet date				
Overdraft at bank				
Profit retained in the business				N/A
Beds in furniture shop				

Item	Asset	Liability	Equity	Type
Beds in residential home				
Deposits received by furniture shop for beds not yet delivered				
Amounts withdrawn by owner of business				N/A

Feedback

Item	Asset	Liability	Equity	Type
Packing machine	✓			Long term
Office computer	✓			Long term
Mortgage on offices		✓		Long term
School building	✓			Long term
Copyright for a song	✓			Long term (intangible)
Pay owed to employee at balance sheet date		✓		Short term
Overdraft at bank		✓		Short term
Profit retained in the business			✓	N/A
Beds in furniture shop	✓			Short term (stock)
Beds in residential home	✓			Long term
Deposits received by furniture shop for beds not yet delivered		✓		Short term
Amounts withdrawn by owner of business			✓	N/A

A repayment mortgage, where some of the loan is repaid each year, should appear both as a short-term liability for the amount due next year and as a long-term liability for the remainder. The balance at a bank is unusual in that it can be either an asset if the account is in the black or not overdrawn, or a liability if it is overdrawn, as here.

'For years, we've been playing by old rules and the results have been dismal. It's time for a bold new direction!'

Finally, it is important to note that accounting statements are reporting events in the past, anything up to a year or more ago by the time the accounts have been prepared and published. But stakeholders need information about the business now and in the future. Balance sheets and the other financial statements are only one of the sources of information available to a stakeholder. In the case of large businesses, for instance public companies listed on stock exchanges, a lot more information is published as and when it is available, showing interim figures (six-monthly or even quarterly), key changes in personnel, new contracts, etc. Stakeholders in a smaller business who have power can demand more information, and more up-to-date information. For instance, the bank can ask Paula to show them her order book and current creditors before granting her an overdraft.

3.7 The cash flow statement

Cash flow is one of the most important aspects of any business. Cash flow should not be confused with profit – they are different concepts. Cash flow shows the money *flowing into* a business from trading receipts, interest received, and any borrowings; and the money *flowing out* of a business through paying for costs, investments in fixed assets, interest, loan repayments and so on.

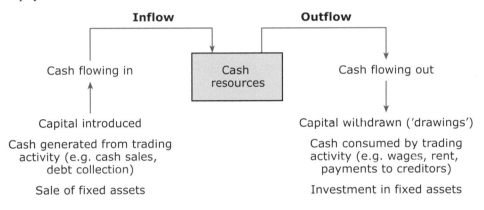

Figure 3.1 Cash inflow and outflows

If the cash flowing into a business does not at least balance the cash flowing out then eventually the business will be unable to meet its debts and could be forced to stop trading. Poor cash flow – represented by more cash flowing out than in – is the single biggest reason why many businesses, especially new businesses, fail. The product or service they are providing may be excellent and the business could be sound in every other way but if cash flow is not managed, the business could fail.

Profit, representing the difference between the revenues and expenses for a particular period, may have little or no relation to the cash generated in the same period. To illustrate this point, let us consider an example.

Peter starts a business with £100. He buys stock, paying the supplier £100. He sells the stock for £200 and agrees that the customer will pay him in three months. He borrows £100 from the bank and buys £200 more stock from a supplier agreeing to pay £100 now and £100 one month later.

Peter's simplified balance sheet now looks like this:

Assets	£	Equity	£
Stock	200	Original capital	100
Debtor	200	Profit earned	100
Total assets	400		
Liabilities			
Bank	100		
Creditor	100		
Total liabilities	200		
Total net assets	200	Total equity	200

Peter has no cash and if his debtor delayed payment he would be unable to repay the bank and pay his creditor. This scenario happens continually with numerous businesses which are apparently profitable but which run out of cash.

The reason for the importance of cash is that people and businesses will normally accept only cash in settlement of their claims against the business. If a business wants to employ people, it must pay them in cash. If it wants to buy a new asset to exploit a business opportunity, the seller of the asset will normally insist on being paid in cash, probably after a short period of credit. When a business fails, it is usually because of its inability to find the cash to pay the amounts owed.

If a business has sufficient cash to draw upon to meet its liabilities as they fall due, it is considered to have good *liquidity*. Surprisingly enough, it is also possible for a business to be too liquid: if it has excess cash for its foreseeable needs then it may not be making best use of its resources. Rather than hoarding cash it might be buying new fixed assets, taking over other businesses or using the cash to fund development projects. In this way the business can expand and become more profitable. Surplus cash not usable in this way might be returned to the business owner for reinvestment elsewhere – although it should be said that different business people will have different views on the level of cash that might be regarded as excess to requirements.

A cash flow statement is therefore a financial statement that ranks in importance alongside the profit and loss account and the balance sheet. Just as a profit and loss account covers a period bracketed by two balance sheets and shows how the change in value of the business (the profit or loss) during that period is explained by reporting revenue and costs, so a cash flow statement shows how cash resources have been generated and consumed during the same period.

You have already seen that there is a generally accepted way of presenting the profit and loss account and balance sheet. There is also a generally accepted format to follow for the cash flow statement, although this format developed in the business world only fairly recently (in the 1970s and 1980s), when some high-profile business failures made the accounting authorities focus on providing more easily understood information, for the benefit of managers and stakeholders, on how businesses generated and consumed their cash resources.

The technical accounting technique for producing a cash flow statement is outside the scope of B120. At this stage in your studies it is sufficient to understand only a summarised version of the format. The information is made more meaningful by grouping the transaction into key headings:

- *Operating activities* are the actions of buying, holding and selling goods, or manufacturing goods for resale, or providing a service to customers, and paying the costs associated with that trading activity.

- *Investing activities* are the actions of buying and selling fixed assets for long-term use or to generate income.

- *Financing activities* are the actions of raising and repaying the long-term finance of the business, and of paying the costs associated with that finance.

Let's look at an example from the small business we are following, Paula's Pipes. We have assumed some figures for Paula's opening balance sheet at 1 January 2008:

Paula's Pipes Cash Flow Statement for the period from 1 January to 31 December 2008

			£
		Operating activity:	
	A	Operating profit before interest on long-term loan	46,800
		Add back non-cash expenses:	
	B	Depreciation	73,000
		Changes in cash invested in Working Capital:	
	C	Increase in Stock (54,300−63,900)	(9,600)
	C	Increase in Debtors (91,500−164,200)	(72,700)
	C	Increase in Prepayments (1,200−1,800)	(600)
	C	Decrease in Creditors (−96,000+95,400)	(600)

D	**Net cash inflow from operating activities**	<u>36,300</u>
	Investing activity:	
E	Investment in Fixed Assets	(20,000)
	Financing activity:	
F	Capital withdrawn ('drawings')	(37,100)
G	**Change in cash balances**	<u>(20,800)</u>
G	**Opening cash balance (overdraft) at 1 January 2008**	(81,900)
G	**Closing cash balance (overdraft) at 31 December 2008**	<u>(102,700)</u>

You will find a cash flow statement together with a profit and loss account and a balance sheet in the published financial statements of any significant business. While it will probably be more complex than the simplified version above, it will follow the same general format. The important points to note are:

(A) Net profit of £46,800 is as reported in the profit and loss account (Session 3.2 above) and represents the primary form of cash generation reported in the cash flow statement.

(B) Depreciation is a cost that does not involve a cash transaction. In order, therefore, to calculate the amount of cash generated by operating activity, depreciation must be added back to profit.

(C) Working capital balances have changed during the accounting period. Each of them represents an investment (or release) of cash resources – for example, if stock levels have increased, the increase must represent some investment of cash in buying extra stock during the period. Similar arguments apply to the other elements of working capital balances.

(D) The cash generated from operating activities (the results of trade and cash amounts invested or released by changes in working capital) is totalled.

(E) Next, investing activities show the amount of cash spent on fixed assets (or, if assets have been sold, the statement shows the amount of cash generated by those sales).

(F) Drawings represent the reduction in capital caused by Paula taking out cash for her own use during the accounting period – this is the same sum as reported in the balance sheet example above.

(G) The final sum of all the above summaries of cash movements is the final change in cash balances during the accounting period which, when added to the opening balance sheet cash position, produces the closing cash position.

Paula's Pipes' cash flow statement tells us something about the business's cash resources that we could not so easily gain from examination of the profit and loss account or the balance sheet. First, we see that cash resources have worsened by £20,800 despite generating a net profit (excluding the non-cash cost of depreciation) of almost £120,000. There are some reasons for this − £20,000 was invested in fixed assets, while Paula removed £37,100 capital for her own use. But we can also clearly see the main reason for this significant difference between the amount of cash generated and the amount of profit earned − the amount of cash invested in debtors has increased by a significant £72,700. Perhaps the first question to ask Paula is whether she is properly chasing up her debtors for the cash they owe her.

3.8 Cash forecasting

Whereas cash flow statements are based on historic (past) events, a cash forecast is essentially a practical exercise where a business is looking ahead to assess not only future income and expenditure but also the level of funding required for a defined period. Key areas to consider include:

- the period of the forecast (3, 6, 12 months)
- the degree of analysis required (weekly, monthly, quarterly)
- the timing of sales revenues
- the relative proportions of cash and credit sales
- potential changes in the level of expenses and the timing of their payment
- the effect of seasonal changes in income and expenditure.

There is no universally agreed way of presenting a cash forecast, but the advantages of the layout shown is that columns are provided for the business owner to insert not only forecast results, but also the actual month's results when they are known. This provides an important means of financial control, as variances between forecast and actual can be investigated and appropriate action taken. No forecast is likely to be wholly accurate; it is the best estimate based on information available at the time of preparation. Some information may be wholly accurate, for example the amount of loan repayments due, or expenditure where the price has been agreed in advance. Other information, such as level of sales income, might be based on a previous year's sales figures with adjustments made for relative decline or increase in trading, etc. A simple cash forecast is shown below. The following is a slightly adapted example:

Cash forecasts for the year to 31 December 2008

	Periods	
	Period 1 £	**Period 2** £
Cash inflow		
A Sales (cash, debtors)		
B Loan received		
C Capital introduced		
D Disposal of assets		
E Total receipts		

	Periods	
	Period 1	**Period 2**
	£	£
Cash outflow		
F Cash purchases		
G Payments to creditors		
H Owner remuneration		
I Wages/salaries		
J PAYE/NI		
K Purchase of fixed assets		
L Transport/packaging		
M Rent/rates		
N Services		
O Loan repayments		
P Interest		
Q Bank/finance charges		
R VAT (Value Added Tax)		
S Corporation/income tax		
T Dividends		
U Total payments		
V Net cash flow (E-U)		
W Opening bank balance		
X Closing bank balance (W±V)		

The explanation for each term is:

(A) Sales – Cash. Some businesses sell for cash at a point of sale. Examples are retail shops bus companies and cinemas. Some businesses are fortunate enough to receive money in advance of providing the service. An example is a travel agency. Some businesses sell on credit (thus creating debtors) where the sale and invoice take place and then payment is received at a later date. The later date can be anything from a few days to many months.

(B) Loan received. This row will only be filled in if loans have been negotiated and money is expected to appear in the bank account.

(C) Capital introduced. The owner(s) of the business will normally introduce actual money into the business at its commencement. Banks normally expect owners to introduce money and not rely solely on bank finance. In the case of companies, capital introduced is usually raised by selling shares in the company. However, many company founders also make loans to the company in addition to buying shares. Note that only money is included in a cash forecasting. Many new business founders introduce other assets (goodwill, motor vehicles, tools, initial stock etc.) but these do not go on a cash flow statement.

(D) Disposal of assets. This is unlikely in a new business. If it does occur only the actual proceeds of sale are included.

(F/G) Cash purchases/creditors. Just as sales can be made for cash or on credit, purchases can be made for cash or on credit. However payments later than desired often occur if the business finds itself short of cash.

(H) Principal(s) remuneration. A person who starts a new business usually has to rely on the business for his or her living expenses and so has to make cash drawings from the business.

(I/J) Wages/salaries. Most employees are paid weekly or monthly and are paid under PAYE (the Pay As You Earn system for paying income tax) and National Insurance. The sum deducted from employees' pay, together with employer's national insurance, is usually paid to the government the month after employees receive their pay.

(K) Fixed assets are assets which are bought for use in the business and not for resale. They have a useful life extending over more than one year. The term capital expenditure is used for the acquisition of fixed assets. In cash forecasting, only the cash payable for the assets is entered.

(L) Transport/packing. Note that a new vehicle will go into row K. This row is for running expenses. Remember that some items are purchased on credit (e.g. a garage bill paid the month following the repair) and the payment goes into the statement in the period it is expected to be paid.

(M) Rent/rates. Rent is often paid quarterly in advance, business rates monthly in arrears.

(N) Services. These may include telephone, gas, electricity and water. Remember that they are payable usually after consumption, either monthly or quarterly.

(O) Loan repayments. Profits have to be large enough to allow for drawings and dividends and loan repayments.

(P) Interest. Banks sometimes charge interest monthly and sometimes quarterly.

(Q) Bank/finance charges. Banking is not free to commercial customers and again bank charges are often negotiable – usually they are paid quarterly.

(R) Value Added Tax. This is usually payable quarterly. VAT is a subject of some complexity and is outside the scope of B120.

(S) Corporation/Income tax. Companies pay corporation tax on their profits after the conclusion of the year in which the profits were earned. The owners of unincorporated business pay income tax on the profits of the businesses. The timing and amount of corporation tax and income tax is a complicated subject and professional advice is essential.

(T) Dividends. Companies can pay dividends to their shareholders. It is unlikely that a new company will declare and pay a dividend until at least the first year is over.

Having entered the payments and receipts for the period, it is necessary to total the amounts in rows E and U. Then the opening cash balance is entered in the first column in row W and the closing balance computed by adding the opening bank balance from the net cash flow to give the month end balance which goes in row X.

A cash forecast is often presented as part of a *business plan*. A business plan can have many different uses, one of which is to present a detailed appraisal of the business to a bank when applying for finance. However, it must not be seen as just a document to show the bank manager and then file away. A regularly updated business plan is an invaluable management tool, allowing performance to be monitored against targets ('forecast' compared with 'actual'), and provides direction for management and staff.

Business plans are usually written for one or more of the following reasons:

- to raise finance, by informing potential lenders or investors about the business
- to identify the business's strengths and weaknesses
- to identify opportunities for expansion and threats to the business's survival
- to set realistic and achievable targets
- to plan the future direction of the business.

Note that a forecast profit and loss account and balance sheet might be included in addition to the cash forecast. This will enable the reader of the plan to assess the anticipated profitability of the business (vital to a future investor) as well as its viability as shown by the change in its net asset position and liquidity as disclosed in the forecast balance sheet.

Activity 3.6

Spend about **30 minutes** on this activity

Purpose: Prepare Paula's Pipes' cash forecast.

Task: It is 31 December 2008. Paula has intentions to expand her business by selling the latest plumbing tools and equipment. Prepare a cash flow forecast for the 3 months to March 2009. Her intentions are:

- She has acquired the lease of a small warehouse, for which she will be paying £5,000 at the beginning of January and an annual rent of £2,400 payable at the end of every quarter, beginning on 31 March, in arrears.
- Gas and electricity costs of £500 in January, £600 in February and £550 in March will appear in the profit and loss account in those months. These are payable in the month following consumption.
- She will buy £12,000 of plumbing equipment in January, £8,000 in February and £8,000 in March. Her supplier expects payment in the month after delivery.
- She will also buy about £400 a month of plumbing tools locally for cash.
- She has arranged to borrow £5,000 in January from her mother repayable at £1,000 a year on December 31 each year. There is no interest on this loan.
- She will put in £4,000 from her own savings, her old van worth £1,500 and her collection of plumbing equipment valued at £2,500.
- She hopes to achieve £800 a month in cash sales, and credit sales of £4,000 in January, £14,000 in February and £16,000 in March. She estimates that payment will be 50% in the month following sale and 50% in the month after that.
- Paula intends to draw £400 a month for herself.
- She will employ Jennifer who will earn £300 a month less £60 income tax. Employers' national insurance will be £30 a month.
- She will need some shelving which will be delivered and paid for in January and cost £7,000. This should last 10 years.
- She will lease a car for herself at a cost of £250 a month.

- She will have to pay professional fees for the warehouse purchase and the cash flow forecast of £600 in February.
- Advertising will be payable in advance at £180 a month. The first adverts will appear in February and be paid for in January.
- We will ignore VAT and any other payments.

Feedback

Paula's Pipes Cash Flow Forecast for the three months to March 2009

	Jan	Feb	Mar	Total
Receipts:				
Loan – mother	5,000			5,000
Capital introduced	4,000			4,000
Cash sales	800	800	800	2,400
Credit sales – receipts		2,000	9,000	11,000
Total	9,800	2,800	9,800	22,400
Payments:				
Lease	5,000			5,000
Rent			600	600
Gas and electricity		500	600	1,100
Creditors		12,000	8,000	20,000
Cash purchases	400	400	400	1,200
Drawings	400	400	400	1,200
Wages	240	240	240	720
PAYE/NHI	90	90	90	270
Shelving	7,000			7,000
Lease of car	250	250	250	750
Professional fees		600		600
Advertising	180	180	180	540
Total	13,560	14,660	10,760	38,980
Change in bank balance	-3,760	-11,860	-960	-16,580
Opening bank balance	-102,700	-106,460	-118,320	-102,700
Closing bank balance	-106,460	-118,320	-119,280	-119,280

Activity 3.7

Spend about **10 minutes** on this activity

Purpose: to test your understanding of cash forecasting.

Task: Answer the following questions by referring to numbers in the previous activity.

Paula is surprised to realise that, despite putting extra money into the company, a larger overdraft would be necessary.

1 Summarise the principal reasons why payments will greatly exceed receipts in the first three month of trading.

2 What would happen if Paula wanted to make payments and the bank overdraft was at or over its limits?

Feedback

1 The principle reasons why payments are greater than receipts in the first three months are:

(a) Paula will need to pay for some items as soon as she starts to expand her business. These include the lease of the warehouse, shelving and equipment.

(b) The company will need to build up a stock which has to be paid for before it is sold.

(c) The company will trade on credit. This means it will buy goods in one month and pay for them at an agreed later date. Most suppliers expect payment in the month following the purchase but frequently find that customers take longer to pay than the agreed time allowed. Similarly Paula has to give credit to her customers. The problem arises because Paula is giving more credit to her customers than her suppliers give to her.

2 She would have to delay making payments until money came in from customers but then other payments may be due. Ultimately being unable to make payments when they fall due can cause a business to go into receivership or liquidation.

3.9 Conclusion

This session examined the main accounting statements produced by businesses: the profit and loss account, the balance sheet and the cash flow statement. We worked through the components of the statements with an example based on Paula's Pipes. You were introduced to the financial matters related to the importance of cash flow in any business. Investigation of the profit and loss account led to some questions about the way accountants define profit. Examination of the way the balance sheet is put together was based on a consideration of the three accounting elements: assets, liabilities and equity. The cash flow statement shows the main sources and uses of cash. Tracking and forecasting the cash movement over several periods may reveal financing and investing patterns and may help guide future management action. We also looked at the relationship between these accounting statements. In the next study session we step back from the technicalities of accounting to look at accounting in its wider context.

3.10 Learning outcomes

By the end of this study session on the main accounting statements you should be able to:

- explain the purpose and format of the three main accounting statements, the profit and loss account, the balance sheet and the cash flow statement;
- understand how the profit and loss account, the balance sheet and the cash flow statement are related to each other;
- describe the five basic accounting elements, and identify and discuss examples of each category.

You will have developed your learning by:

- applying your learning about the main accounting statements to the small-business example of Paula's Pipes.

Session 4 The accounting world

Why are we studying 'the accounting world'? In order to have a better understanding of why accountants prepare accounting statements in the way they do, and of the different branches of accounting, we need to spend some time considering the world within which accountancy and accountants operate. This will help us set accounting record-keeping in its context, and may also help explain the image that accountants often have in the eyes of the general public.

The **aims and objectives** of Session 4 are to:

- describe the framework of accounting concepts within which the accounting statements are prepared;
- examine the different branches of accounting, and consider the differences between financial accounting and management accounting;
- look at how the information produced by accountants is regulated, and consider the part played by professional accountancy bodies in this process;
- think about the image that accountancy, and accountants, have in the eyes of the general public.

4.1 The conceptual framework of accounting

In drawing up accounting statements, whether they are external financial accounts or internally-focused management accounts, a clear objective has to be that the accounts fairly reflect the true substance of the business and the results of its operation.

The theory of accounting has, therefore, developed the concept of a *true and fair view*. The true and fair view is applied in ensuring and assessing whether accounts do indeed accurately portray the business' activities.

To support the application of the true and fair view, accounting has adopted certain concepts which help to ensure that accounting information is presented accurately and consistently.

Underlying accounting concepts

A number of underlying accounting concepts have been applied ever since financial statements were first produced for external reporting purposes. They are generally reinforced through custom and practice, rather than through regulation or legislation.

The historical cost concept

Assets are normally shown in the financial statements at a value based on their original cost. This is objective because it is based on actual invoices and other documents. If you bought a PC for £1,000, you would have received an invoice or receipt for £1,000. This receipt is objective evidence of the cost of the PC. Thus Paula's van will appear in her balance sheet at its original cost, less depreciation.

The money measurement concept

Accounting information has traditionally been concerned only with:

- those facts that can be measured in financial terms; and
- those transactions whose financial value most people will agree to.

Quite simply, because it is impossible to put financial values on everything, financial statements don't tell us everything about a business. For example, although the financial statements should show the value of all the financial assets and liabilities of the business, they do not show:

- whether the firm has good or bad managers;
- if there are serious problems with the workforce;
- if a rival product is about to take away many of its best customers;
- if the government is about to pass a law which will cost the business a lot of extra expense in future.

This is because the money measurement concept cannot successfully capture issues such as these. The overall implication is that, regardless of the identity of the end user of the financial statements, the financial statements should be seen as just one of a series of items of information required before any serious decisions should be taken.

The business entity concept

Accountants keep the affairs of a business totally separate from the non-business activities of its owners. The items recorded in the accounting records or books of the business are therefore restricted to the transactions of the business. No matter what activities the proprietor(s) participate in outside the business, these are completely disregarded in the accounting records kept by the business. It is mainly for this reason that funds or goods taken out of a business by its owners are treated as a reduction in their investment in the business, not as an expense of the business. This is illustrated in the example below.

Example 4.1

Some years ago a local transport provider (let's call them BusCo) applied for a subsidy for some little-used but vital routes. The subsidy provider asked to see the figures that proved that the subsidy was needed. Unfortunately BusCo also ran a garage, and the accounts for the two activities were not kept separate. Just how confused the accounts were became clear when the subsidy provider's accountant lent a hand to split the figures between the two enterprises. They found various expenses that had been met from the business bank accounts that were nothing to do with the business, including vet's bills and dog food. The errors had arisen because the accounts had been prepared from the bank statements, and, as well as combining accounts for different activities, BusCo had also used the business cheque books for personal expenses. In order to maintain clarity, businesses are urged by their accountants to keep bank accounts separate. In this case, the owner was one accounting entity, BusCo was another and the garage was a third.

The dual aspect concept

Every transaction is seen as having two aspects, one represented by changes to the assets of the business and the other by changes to the claims against them, those claims being liabilities and equity. The dual aspect concept states that these two aspects are always equal to each other. This is the basis of double entry, a method of bookkeeping in which there are two entries for each transaction, one called a debit and the other called a credit, that check and balance each other. We looked at the principles of double-entry bookkeeping in Section 2.4.

The time interval concept

One of the underlying principles of accounting is that financial statements are prepared at regular intervals, usually of one year. For companies, financial statements and supporting information, including a report from the company chairman and another from the company auditor, will appear in the annual financial report. For internal management purposes accounting statements may be prepared more frequently, often on a monthly basis or even more often.

Fundamental accounting concepts

Now we turn to fundamental accounting concepts. These tend to be enforced through regulation and legislation. In the UK fundamental accounting concepts are covered by *accounting standards* and are known by the acronym GAAP in the UK (Generally Accepted Accounting Principles). Accounting standards are a series of pronouncements by the accountancy profession which must be followed by qualified accountants in preparing financial statements. They supplement and reinforce the provisions of company law, which can tend to lag behind current best professional practice.

Going concern

When preparing financial statements, values are based on the assumption that the business will continue to operate for the foreseeable future. This may seem to be hardly worth saying, but in some cases it could make a big difference to values. If a business has a highly specialised asset that is useful only for producing specific items, it may be worth very little to others. So if the business were going to close down, it would be necessary to review the value of that asset in the financial statements.

The accruals concept

We looked at this concept in study Sessions 2 and 3 of this book when considering the difference between cash accounting and the more usual accrual accounting which is used to prepare financial statements. Remember that accrual accounting requires that income and expenses appear in the financial statements of the period in which they were earned or incurred, and that they be matched in order to arrive at the profit (or loss) for the period. Therefore, where expenditure has been incurred during a period for which revenue or benefit has not yet been received, the expenditure should be omitted from the calculation of profit for that period and carried forward to the period when the revenue or benefit results. An example would be annual buildings insurance paid mid-period that is valid for the first six months of the next period. This also applies in reverse when the benefit is received before the expenditure occurs. An example would be electricity consumed before a period end and not yet charged by the supplier, as the billing date for electricity is after the period end. We considered examples of these two types of adjustment in study Session 3 in the context of Paula's Pipes.

Consistency

Each item should be treated in the same way in every period, as far as possible.

There are a number of different ways in which some accounting concepts can be applied. Each business should choose the approach that gives the most reliable picture of the business, not just for this period, but also over time. The consistency concept says that when a method has been adopted for the accounting treatment of an item, the same method should be adopted for all subsequent occurrences of similar items. This should be the case not just within an accounting period, but also between subsequent accounting periods. So if Paula buys a new van she should use the same method of depreciation that was used for the old van. A more contentious issue is whether different businesses should be made to use the same methods. This is one of the issues that accounting standards, mentioned above, are trying to deal with.

Prudence

This implies that the accountant should always be prudent when preparing financial statements. In other words, if something is in doubt, the accountant should assume the worst and, if a transaction has not yet been completed, the accountant should ignore any benefits that may arise from it. Assets should not be valued too highly. Nor should amounts owed by a business be understated. Otherwise, people might be misled into lending to or granting credit to a business when they would not have done had they known the true facts. The prudence concept requires that all losses (costs) are recognised immediately they become known whereas all gains (revenue) should be recognised only when they are realised (certain to be received). As a result, profits will normally be understated. It could be argued that this is not particularly helpful for the economic decisions of users, and a more well-balanced view might be appropriate. However, from other perspectives, for example paying tax, it is more understandable.

Substance over form

Each transaction should be included in the financial statements in a way that shows its economic impact on the business. The legal form of a transaction may differ from its real substance. Where this happens, accounting should show the transaction in accordance with its real substance, that is, according to how the transaction affects the economic situation of the firm. This means that accounting may not reflect the exact legal position concerning that transaction.

The idea of substance over form most frequently applies to leases and hire purchase transactions. Take the example of a machine being acquired by hire purchase. Legally, it does not belong to the business until the last instalment is paid and an option has been taken up by the business to become the owner of the machine. Clearly, however, hire purchase is used by businesses to purchase assets in stages, and the business has used the machine since it first acquired it in the same way as it would have done had it paid for it in full at the outset. The substance-over-form concept says that the business should show the full value of the machine being bought on hire purchase in its financial statements as though it were legally owned by the business as an asset, and show the full amount still owing to the supplier of the machine separately as a liability.

Materiality

The accounting concepts discussed above have been assimilated over many years, and they are now accepted in the business world. However, there is one over-riding rule applied to anything that appears in a financial accounting statement – that it should be material. That is, it should be of interest to stakeholders – the people who make use of financial accounting statements. We discussed materiality in study Session 1. Businesses make their own judgements to determine what is material and what is not. There is no law or regulation in the UK that defines these rules – the decision on what is material and what is not is a matter of judgement. A business may decide that all items under £200 should be treated as expenses in the period in which they were bought even though they may be used for the following ten years. Another business may fix the limit at £500. Different limits may be set for different types of item. The larger the business, the larger the limits tend to be. For an individual, paying £10,000 for a new car may be beyond their ability. A multi-millionaire, on the other hand, wouldn't think twice about spending that amount on a first-class air ticket. To the multi-millionaire, £10,000 is immaterial, for the average person, it is material. Businesses are the same. What is expensive and very significant for small businesses may be cheap and insignificant for larger ones.

4.2 Value

There is an aspect to the definition of the five basic accounting elements we looked at in Section 3.6 of this book that has not yet been discussed. In order for an item to appear in the accounts it has to have a value, and stakeholders using the accounts must be able to understand and rely on that value. But for many things there may be more than one potential valuation.

We can use the following example of a town centre clock to consider the concept of value. Read the example and then do Activity 4.1.

Example 4.2

There was a building in a Scottish town centre that had been built many years ago and used ever since as a jeweller's shop. On the side of the building, jutting out into the high street, was a large clock, which told the time to anyone travelling up or down the street. Generations of local shoppers had grown up using this clock to tell them when they had to go back to work or catch their bus home. In the 1980s the jewellers closed and the building was sold. The new owners wanted to demolish and rebuild, and the clock had no place in the new plans. There was an outcry, led by the local paper, and much discussion about the need to keep the clock in position. Various options were considered – no clock, putting a modern clock face into the new building, moving the original clock to another street. Eventually the town council undertook to mount the clock on a property they owned on the other side of the street, where it would be as visible as it had been in the original position. The question arose, just how much was the clock worth? Should the council pay the new owners of the building for the clock? And, if so, how much? Whether or not they paid for the clock, it was an asset to the town, so what value should be recorded in their accounts?

The jeweller had the original records of purchase, which showed the clock had been made for them for a sum of £5. When the building had been sold the price was inclusive of the clock. The estimate for the modern replacement was £100 plus installation costs of £400. The

> estimate for moving the original clock was at least £1,000. An estimate of the cost of buying and installing a similar clock made in the same way was £10,000. All these figures could be seen as potential values for the clock. As it turned out, the new owners donated the clock to the council. This was not so much an accounting decision as a public relations activity. The council then incurred £800 in moving the clock to its new position.

Having read the above example, what value do you think the council should have recorded in their accounts for the clock and why?

There are several possible answers to this question. If the council considered that their asset was basically a timepiece providing a service to the public, then the appropriate valuation might be the cheapest way of providing that service. That could be done with the modern replacement at a total of £500.

If the council considered that what they had was a piece of local history that provided the time as a public service then a valuation might have to take into account the cost of replacing the clock with a new but similar one at £10,000. If the council considered that they had an antique, they could have had it valued and recorded it at that price, ignoring the service it provided. However, the figure that was used for the asset was the cost to the council, which was the £800 it had cost to install.

4.3 Branches of accounting

Activity 4.1

Spend about **90 minutes** on this activity

Purpose: to clarify your understanding of the different types and branches of accounting.

Task: read Essential Reading 2 'Branches of accounting' by John Dyson (2004) which you will find at the back of this book. Make notes as you go along.

Feedback

The main aim of this book is to introduce you, as a non-accountant, to the world and central practices of accountancy. From your reading of and note taking on Essential Reading 2 you should appreciate that there are five main branches of accounting: financial accounting/reporting, management accounting, auditing, taxation and financial management. Two sub-branches are bookkeeping and cost bookkeeping. Ensure that you understand the differences between them. The next section should help.

Now that you have completed Essential Reading 2, we can clarify further the differences between financial accounting and management accounting within a business.

4.4 The difference between financial and management accounting

Management accounting provides the managers *within* a business with the information to help them make planning and control decisions. The preparation of accounting reports mainly for *external* use is called financial accounting. It is important to realise that both types of accounting might use the same original information for different purposes.

Managers are most concerned with accounting information that helps them to protect the assets of the business, to make sound plans and to control the activities of the business, and that aids them with general decision making and strategy. Unlike financial accounting, which is primarily public information, management accounting is primarily for confidential use within a business.

Financial accounting, on the other hand, is concerned with preparing accounting information for the benefit of all the other financial stakeholders of a business, mainly outside, but also inside, the business. These financial stakeholders are most concerned with the overall profit of the business, its financial value, and its social and environmental impact.

Table 4.1 summarises the main differences between management accounting and financial accounting.

Table 4.1 Differences between management accounting and financial accounting

Management accounting	Financial accounting
A management accounting system produces information that is mainly used for management purposes within an organisation	A financial accounting system produces information that is mainly used by parties external to the organisation
Management accounting helps management to record, plan and control activities and aids the decision-making process	Financial accounting provides a record of the performance of an organisation over a financial year and the financial value at the end of that financial year
There are no legal requirements for an organisation to use management accounting	Limited liability companies must, by law, prepare financial accounts
Management accounting can focus on specific areas of a business's activities	Financial accounting concentrates on the whole organisation, aggregating revenues and costs from different operations
Management accounting provides both a historical record of the immediate past and a future planning tool	Financial accounting presents an essentially historical picture of past operations
Accounting statements are produced as a once-off and also for varying periods	Accounting statements are normally required to be produced for a period of 12 months
No strict rules govern the way in which management accounting operates	Financial accounting must operate within a framework determined by law and international and/or national accounting standards
Management accounting has no specified format and no specific, required statements	Financial accounts are supposed to be produced in accordance with a format specified by accounting standards and by law

Because financial accounting is a legal requirement, it sets a framework for all the accounts within a business. As a result, if parts of a business have to report to the headquarters they will probably be expected to use the same principles as the business as a whole uses for the financial statements. The recording of transactions within the business will be set up to produce the financial accounts that are mandatory. So any other use of the accounting information has to elicit details from a structure that was designed primarily for another purpose. Sophisticated accounting information systems can produce two or more completely different analyses of information from the same basic transactions recorded in the business's accounting database. However, in many businesses even if this feature is available it is underdeveloped, and management accounting is often done using spreadsheets for specific, discrete bits of analysis. The problem in Example 4.3 arose when a new financial information system was installed for a hospital group.

Example 4.3

When potential suppliers came to sell a new computer system to the users of the financial information system, one feature of the new system that impressed the users was its ability to record information in many different ways. For example, it was possible to set up a repair job for the laundry in one hospital and then put the cost of the job into maintenance costs for that hospital or into the costs of the laundry service. The finance staff could add up the costs for all the hospitals or the costs for all the services to give the costs for the business as a whole. This meant that they could report to the board by hospital. They could also report to the budget managers for the laundry service and to the maintenance managers on the costs and components of individual jobs.

When the new system was installed a lot of information had to be fed in to build the structure for generating reports. The constraints on time available meant that the financial reporting structure was prioritised, and then, over the next year, the reporting to the laundry managers was set up. The initialisation of the job-costing system was left until last, and meanwhile the maintenance managers just carried on with their spreadsheet system. Because the information for this was fed in manually some costs got left out, which led to conflict about which system was right. Because the maintenance managers saw the new system as giving 'wrong' information they had an excuse to avoid using the costing system, which also saved them the effort of doing the initialisation.

We have included this real-life example to show how, in this case, financial reporting was seen as more important, and so tended to dominate decisions about management accounting. It also illustrates some behavioural issues about accounting information.

- People can be possessive with accounting information.
- People prefer to keep existing systems rather than change to new ones.
- Effort required to change accounting methods or content has to be balanced by an improvement in the resulting accounting figures that are actually used by the people who have to make the effort.
- When two systems are producing different answers to the same question the people concerned will defend their own system as being more correct.

These points also apply to non-accounting systems of course, but there are aspects of accounting that can magnify any problem they cause.

Accounting is not the main task of most people in a business; they are busy selling, making, delivering, etc. Form filling or computer work that is not seen as directly contributing to their task tends to take second place and can be resented for the time it takes away from their main job. We mentioned the need for reconciliation of information being run on separate systems (manual or computerised) in Section 2.4. The problem with reconciliation is that it is an extra task, and is not welcomed by staff who think that their own system is producing the correct figures anyway. Accountants sometimes fail to see that reconciliation of figures is not the first priority of other staff and can become upset about their colleagues' lack of interest.

Many people think that numbers are difficult, and they may see information based on numbers as more scientific and therefore more likely to be right. Management accounting, particularly budget preparation and monitoring, is used for control purposes in businesses, so possession of this accounting information can confer power on the holder. The maintenance team that produced their own job-costing information at the hospital used it to prove that they had not overspent their budgets. They were (rightly as it turned out) worried that the new financial information system would show them as overspending.

Activity 4.2

Spend about **15 minutes** on this activity

Purpose: to reinforce your understanding of the difference between management accounting and financial accounting.

Task: based on your understanding so far, fill in the table below according to whether you think the accounting information or statement (on the left-hand side) refers mainly to management accounting or financial accounting.

Accounting information or statement	Management accounting or financial accounting
The profit earned by a business in a financial year	
The equity of a business at the end of the financial year	
The cost of producing and/or selling a particular product or range of products	
The cost of running a particular part of a business	
The profit earned by part of a business on a month-by-month basis	
The quantity of a product which must be sold in order for it to cover its expenses	
The amount of cash coming into and leaving a business in a financial year	
The expected overdraft requirements of a business at defined intervals in the financial year	
The cash flow statement	
The cash flow forecast	
The sales forecast	

Feedback

After some reflection on the different accounting information needs of managers and other stakeholders, you should have come up with the following.

Accounting information or statement	Management accounting or financial accounting
The profit earned by a business in a financial year	Financial accounting
The equity of a business at the end of the financial year	Financial accounting
The cost of producing and/or selling a particular product or range of products	Management accounting
The cost of running a particular part of a business	Management accounting
The profit earned by part of a business on a month-by-month-basis	Management accounting
The quantity of a product which must be sold in order for it to cover its expenses	Management accounting
The amount of cash coming into and leaving a business in a financial year	Financial accounting
The expected overdraft requirements of a business at defined intervals in the financial year	Management accounting
The cash flow statement	Financial accounting
The cash flow forecast	Management accounting
The sales forecast	Management accounting

4.5 The accounting profession and regulation

There are various sources of regulation that determine what information accountants must include in published accounting statements. We noted in Section 4.4 that the law plays a role in determining the type of information that must be included in accounting statements prepared for external users. In the UK there is a well-established body of company law that, among other things, sets out fairly detailed requirements for the content and format of the published accounting statements produced by limited companies. However, the accounting profession also gets involved with this area.

As outlined in Essential Reading 2, the accounting profession in the UK consists of six different organisations:

- The Institute of Chartered Accountants in England and Wales (ICAEW)
- The Institute of Chartered Accountants in Ireland (ICAI).
- The Institute of Chartered Accountants of Scotland (ICAS)
- Association of Chartered Certified Accountants (ACCA)
- The Chartered Institute of Management Accountants (CIMA)
- The Chartered Institute of Public Finance and Accountancy (CIPFA)

These bodies belong to the Consultative Committee of Accountancy Bodies (CCAB) and each one holds its own examinations for membership.

One of the functions of the UK professional bodies that has developed in recent years is the preparation and promulgation of accounting standards. These can be seen as authoritative statements which codify the practice of financial accounting, and which members of the professional bodies are required to comply with. The main purpose of accounting standards is to narrow down the range of acceptable accounting methods in line with current best practice. Some standards are sector- or size-specific and some more general.

Every country has its own standards, and although the basic principles are mostly the same there are significant differences. As a result of this and the increased globalisation of larger businesses and finance there has been a move towards internationalisation of standards. The International Accounting Standards Board has created an additional layer of standards. These International Financial Reporting Standards (IFRSs) are being adopted or worked towards by most of the larger economies. IFRSs were created in response to the needs of international investors and companies to be able to understand financial information from other countries. Because of this they are primarily designed for the owners of and investors in large, public, listed companies. As a result, the original set of IFRSs did not fit particularly well with private companies, smaller companies or other sectors. At the time of writing, the UK, in common with many other countries, requires public companies with shares or debt listed on stock exchanges to use IFRSs, whereas other businesses can use either domestic standards or IFRSs. The status and content of accounting standards undergoes frequent modification, as standards are reviewed, consulted upon, changed and then adopted. During the introduction and adoption of IFRSs this change process accelerated.

Another source of rules for financial statements is the oversight and authority bodies. In the UK the most significant body for publicly quoted companies is the Financial Services Authority, which sets the rules that apply to companies listed on UK stock exchanges. These rules are in addition to accounting standards and the law, and demand more disclosure of information, for instance half-yearly financial statements. Public-sector entities that are audited by Audit Scotland or the Accounts Commission or the Audit Commission or the National Audit Office (for England and Wales) may have to follow particular formats or supply particular information specified by the auditing body as being best practice. Charities in England and Wales are required to follow the rules of the Charities Commission. There are also regulatory bodies in particular fields. For example, health boards must complete their accounts in a format set down by the NHS; and churches may be required to follow rules set by their synod. In addition to all these requirements, branches of large organisations will have to follow rules set by the head office, and companies may have to follow practice set down by a parent company.

The point we are making is that there is more than one set of rules, and what applies to one business may not apply to the next. So how on earth can stakeholders read and understand sets of accounts that may be so different? It is not quite as bad as it seems. First, a lot of the rules apply to layout and terminology rather than principles, so an understanding of the basic accounting elements and main financial statements should allow interpretation of many different styles of accounts. Second, the notes to the accounts should always include a section on accounting policies. If the accounts contain any significant departure from normal accounting this should be explained in the accounting policies. The idea of 'comply or explain' has become standard for all sectors.

Activity 4.3

Spend about **45 minutes** on this activity

Purpose: to view some of the websites of some professional accounting institutions in the country where you live.

Task: use an internet search engine such as Google or Yahoo! to find and explore the web pages of one or more of the accounting bodies in the UK or elsewhere. Try to get a feel for the types of activity they get involved with on behalf of their members.

4.6 The image of accountancy

Many people, including business studies students, feel uncomfortable about accounting. The traditional view is that the main purpose of accounting is merely keeping track of money and profit. Accountants are seen as dealing with numbers, facts and quantitative data, and have a fairly negative stereotypic image as Example 4.4 on the next page shows.

Example 4.4

If it feels like accountancy has taken a hammering in the national press like no other sector figures prepared for *Accountancy Age* this week confirm it.

In terms of negative press coverage over the past 12 months, accountancy ranks a distant 45th out of the 45 leading UK business sectors. Accountants fared worse than banks, telecoms companies and estate agents, according to the PressWatch index, which measures the balance of positive and negative publicity ...

Ernst & Young, which endured a hard time over its handling of the Equitable Life audit, scored minus 105; KPMG (accused of violating auditor independence rules) scored minus 362; whilst PricewaterhouseCoopers (criticised for its audit of Russia's biggest company Gazprom) scored minus 438.

Not surprisingly, Andersen's demise hurt accountancy the most. The firm scored minus 5,133 making it the worst performing of all UK companies assessed. It was run close by Marconi.

But there was some good news in the figures. Since Andersen's collapse, the sector has begun to recover. Recent figures show accountancy climbed back up to a comparatively respectable 36th out of 43 in September.

(Source: Wild, 2002, quoted in Dyson, 2004, p. 2)

The media love a good story about accounting 'scandals'. People do not really understand what accountants do and why they cost so much, so it is not surprising that they are often treated with suspicion.

Complete Activity 4.4, which consists of three stages. Each of these stages should take about an hour of your allotted time for this book. This activity and Activity 4.5 which follows must be completed before B120 Day School 2.

Activity 4.4

Spend about **3 hours** on this activity

Purpose: to use a recent example of an accounting scandal to explore the image of accountancy.

Task: complete the three stages below.

1   Think of a specific example of a well-publicised accounting scandal somewhere in the world in the recent past. You will need to find a case for sharing at the forthcoming B120 day school. Use the internet to explore any recent news stories or type in the search words 'accounting scandals'.

2   Post a brief summary of your chosen example on your tutor group forum. Your tutor will indicate the appropriate time to do this. Everyone in your group will be asked to submit an example they have found. Using the shared examples on the tutor group forum, participate in an online, collaborative discussion on why accounting scandals occur. Your tutor will contribute to the tutor group forum to guide your thinking and shared discussion. For example, were the examples of accounting scandals found based on fraud, human error or some other factor? Who seemed to be to blame for the scandals? External auditors? Company directors? Company accountants? The media? Or someone else?

3   Read the short extract from Dyson (2004) in Example 4.5. Make notes as
    you go along.

Feedback

These activities will form the basis of the exercise on accounting and finance
in Day School 2. Please complete the activities and bring your notes to the
day school.

Example 4.5

Why accounting is important for non-accountants

We assume that as a non-accountant student you aim to become a
senior manager in some entity (accountants use the term *entity* to mean
any type of organization). That entity might be profit-making, e.g. a
company selling goods and services, or a not-for-profit entity, such as a
charity or a government department.

At a more junior level your work might be fairly routine, it may not be
very demanding and you might have little responsibility. As you become
more experienced and competent you may be promoted to a more
responsible post. Alternatively, you may already hold a senior post but
one perhaps of a technical nature. For example, you might be in charge
of a chemical laboratory or one of the company's engineering sections.
Nevertheless, your present duties may be restricted to the technical
aspects of the job and you may not be involved in the wider aspects of
running the entity.

That position will change as you become more senior. You will become
much more involved in the planning of the entity, the control of its
resources, and in taking an active part in decision-making, i.e. in
determining its future.

In performing such duties you will be supplied with a great deal of
information relating to the administrative, production and sales functions
of the entity. Such technical information will have been stored, extracted,
summarized and translated into a language that all managers are
expected to understand. That language is called *accounting* and hence
accounting is often referred to as the language of business. By using a
common language managers can understand each other without it being
necessary for them to become an expert in the other functions of an
entity.

But, as a manager, what accounting information will be given to you?
What are you expected to do with it? Is it given to you just because it
might be of interest?

... As far as the last question is concerned, the simple answer is 'no'.
You are given that information for a purpose. You are supposed to do
something with it. But what?

In broad terms, there are three main functions that, as a senior manager, you will be expected to undertake. The accounting information that you receive should help you to carry out such functions more effectively. In summary, they are as follows:

1 *Planning.* As a manager you will be a vital member of the management team responsible for both the long-term and the short-term planning of the entity.

2 *Control.* You will use the entity's agreed long- and short-term plans to help you control the day-to-day activities of the entity.

3 *Decision making.* You will use the information to make decisions about the entity's progress and its long-term future, e.g. whether to invest in a new factory or close down a loss-making unit.

In order to help you carry out these functions you will be supplied with and will come to depend upon the type of information prepared by your accounting team. The information will obviously not mean much to you if you do not understand it. It would be like receiving reports written in French if you did not know a word of French. So you need to be reasonably fluent in speaking accounting. Otherwise, you will not be able to communicate with your fellow managers and you might be taking decisions based on information that means nothing to you.

The relationship between accounting information and the use management makes of it is shown in Figure 4.1 [below].

There is another reason why you need to know something about accounting. In most types of entities there is a legal obligation placed upon you as a senior manager to comply with various statutory accounting provisions. It would be very unwise, therefore, if you ignored your legal responsibilities and you did not take the necessary steps to ensure that you did as the law required. Ignorance of the law is no excuse for breaking it.

At this point you might be thinking along the following lines:

> OK, I accept that accounting is an important subject but I still don't really see why I have to know much about it. The accountants can't tell me how to do my job and they will make sure that I follow the legal requirement. All that number crunching that accountants do is a waste of time as far as I am concerned.

You might have a point. It may not be absolutely essential for you to do much 'number crunching' but it does give you a better idea of where the information comes from and what it means. If you are familiar with its source then you will be able to judge much more keenly how much reliance to place on it.

In summary, therefore, we would argue that accounting is a vital subject for non-accountants to study because, as a manager:

1 it will help you to take more meaningful and effective decisions based on information that you have been able to check; and

2   you can ensure that the entity carries out its legal obligations.

(Source: Dyson, 2004, pp. 4–6)

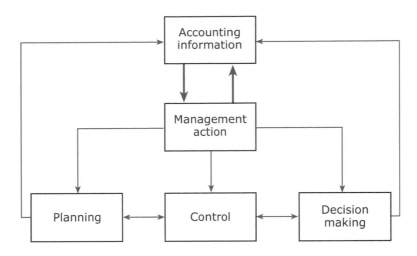

Figure 4.1 The relationship between accounting information and management

Activity 4.5

Spend about **1 hour** on this activity

Purpose: to reflect on how to improve the image of accountancy.

Task: using the notes you have made and the thinking you have done in Activity 4.4, prepare the basis of a short (no more than 5 minutes) presentation at the forthcoming B120 day school on the two questions below:

1   Why do accountants tend to have a negative image?

2   How can this image be made more positive, given the importance of accounting to business?

Feedback

To help you complete this activity think about what accounting does and why accounting is so important for businesses and for most employees, including non-accountants. Use the examples of accounting scandals that you and other students have posted on the tutor group forum to help your thinking. At the day school this will be a group presentation not an individual one, but you will need to be prepared and to contribute.

4.7 Conclusion

This session looked at the world inhabited by accountants and accountancy. It is important that you realise that accounting is a human invention, and the study of it is essentially a branch of the social sciences. To understand properly what accountants do, and why, we need to look at the world of accounting. In this session we looked at the conceptual framework of accounting – the ground rules that have grown up over time and through practice and custom. We then examined the different branches of accounting, with particular emphasis on the differences between financial accounting and management accounting. The outputs of the process of financial accounting, often known as financial reporting, are regulated for many business entities, and we reviewed the main components of the regulatory system. Finally we spent some time thinking about the image that accountancy and accountants have when viewed from the perspective of outsiders. In the next, final, study session we look at budgets and the budgeting process.

4.8 Learning outcomes

By the end of this study session on the accounting world you should be able to:

- understand the main accounting concepts that surround the preparation of the accounting statements;
- appreciate the different branches of accounting and explain the main differences between financial accounting and management accounting;
- describe the regulatory processes that govern the production of accounting information produced for public consumption;
- offer your views on the often negative image that the general public has of accountants and accountancy.

You will have developed your learning by:

- seeing how the accounting concepts introduced in the study session apply to real-life business examples;
- using the internet to find out more about different professional accounting bodies.

Session 5 Budgets and the budgeting process

Why are we studying 'budgets and the budgeting process'? We have spent some time in previous study sessions considering how and why businesses prepare financial reports for external users. Now we need to consider what goes on inside the business. It could be argued that this is even more important than producing reports for those outside.

The **aims and objectives** of Session 5 are to:

- describe what budgeting is and why it is important for businesses;
- outline how the budgeting process works;
- look at different types of cost and how they behave in relation to changes in the level of business activity;
- consider the behavioural implications of budgeting.

5.1 Budgets and budgetary control

If a business does not produce high-quality accounting information for internal use, it is in danger of being poorly run and may get into financial difficulties. Some research carried out in the 1990s (Day and Taylor, 2002, p. 130) observed a clear link between poor-quality management accounting information and financial distress in small- and medium-sized enterprises, although we should note that it was not possible to determine the direction of causality. It might have been poor accounting information that led to financial difficulties, or it might have been financial difficulties that led to poor accounting information, or some other characteristic of the business or its operating conditions may have led to both poor accounting information and financial difficulties.

Let's consider some formal definitions of *budgets* and budgeting, and look at how the budgeting process works.

Activity 5.1

Spend about **45 minutes** on this activity

Purpose: to consider what is meant by a budget and a budgeting process.

Task: read Essential Reading 3 'Budgeting and budgetary control' by John Dyson, which you will find at the back of this book. Take notes as you go along.

Feedback

This study session aims to show you the importance of budgets and budgeting for all sizes and types of business. Your reading of Essential Reading 3 and the notes you made should have helped you understand why businesses prepare budgets and how they go about it. You should also have learned how budgets are used to exercise financial control over business operations. The next section considers this with some practical examples.

5.2 Preparing and using budgets

Most employees do not get involved in producing the financial accounts and may never see them. But they will hear about or see a budget in all but the smallest business. A budget is a financial plan. It can be seen as a statement of the financial effects expected from the resource conversion processes that the business has planned. For instance, to set a budget for cash inflows and outflows for Sue's travel agency (which we looked at in study Session 1) for the coming year, Sue would have to estimate the value of holidays that she expects to sell to her customers, so that expected cash inflows from commission can be worked out. She would also have to estimate her expenses for the period concerned to get figures for anticipated cash outflows. Does this sound familiar? Look back at Activity 1.3 in study Session 1, where you prepared a simple budget. It really can be that easy. This information helped Sue to estimate the year's anticipated cash inflow for her business, and would have enabled her to plan what to do about repaying her bank loan. Sue can also use these figures to monitor what actually happens as the year progresses, by making a comparison of actual figures against her plan.

One thing that would help Sue to both plan and monitor would be to have her budget set out on a monthly basis. We will use this as the basis for Activity 5.2.

Activity 5.2

Spend about **30 minutes** on this activity

Purpose: to understand how budgets can be used to help owners and/or managers plan and control their business's operations.

Task: consider the information set out below on Sue's travel agency, and answer the questions which follow.

With Gavin's help, Sue converted her rough budget for the travel agency's cash inflows and outflows for the coming year into a monthly budget:

£ thousands	Jan	Feb	Mar	Apr	May	Jun
Cash in:						
Commission	10	10	10	10	5	5
Cash out:						
Regular expenses	5	5	5	5	5	5
Sue's drawings	2.5	2.5	2.5	2.5	2.5	2.5
ATOL/insurance	–	–	–	–	–	–
	7.5	7.5	7.5	7.5	7.5	7.5
Surplus/deficit	2.5	2.5	2.5	2.5	–2.5	–2.5
Previous month's balance	–	2.5	5	7.5	10	7.5
New balance	2.5	5	7.5	10	7.5	5

£ thousands	Jul	Aug	Sep	Oct	Nov	Dec
Cash in:						
Commission	5	5	10	10	10	10
Cash out:						
Regular expenses	5	5	5	5	5	5
Sue's drawings	2.5	2.5	2.5	2.5	2.5	2.5
ATOL/insurance	–	1.5	–	–	–	–
	7.5	9	7.5	7.5	7.5	7.5
Surplus/deficit	–2.5	–4	2.5	2.5	2.5	2.5
Previous month's balance	5	2.5	–1.5	1	3.5	6
New balance	2.5	–1.5	1	3.5	6	8.5

1   First, spend five minutes studying this information. Make sure that you understand the figures, and where they come from (you will find it helpful to refer back to Activity 1.3 in study Session 1).

2   Does the information as now presented tell you anything new? What do you think are the important points that Sue should take note of?

3   Can you make a few suggestions for Sue that might help her avoid any problems caused by the pattern of cash flows revealed by the monthly budget?

Feedback

1   The information above takes Sue's annual figures and presents them month by month. This is how she first obtained the information. The figures are presented to show total cash coming in, and total cash going out. The difference between these two figures is then that month's surplus or deficit, and when the previous month's balance is added in, we get the new cash balance at the end of the month.

2   It does tell us something new. It shows quite clearly that, if things go according to plan, Sue will have a minor cash flow crisis in August and she needs to plan how to deal with this. It is caused by the ATOL and insurance payments that she needs to make in August, which come at a time of the year when business is relatively slack and cash inflows low. However, excluding the issue of repaying her £10,000 bank loan, the business has a good cash flow over the year as a whole.

3 There are various things that Sue could do to deal with this. Her business is significantly seasonal, and there is probably not much she can do about her cash inflows in the short term. Her regular expenses are also not likely to be easy to change in the short term. However, she may well have more control over the remaining items in the budget. Some suggestions are listed below.

- First, she should see if she can pay the ATOL subscription and insurance premium at a time of year when monthly cash flow is positive, perhaps the end of the year. Paying in August, when business is slack, is bound to cause a problem for her.

- If this is not possible, she could request payment by instalments.

- It is not just the ATOL and insurance payments that are causing the problem. Sue's personal drawings are also an area for review. It would improve the business's cash flow over the slack summer months if she took out less cash then (and perhaps compensated by taking out more during the rest of the year). She doesn't necessarily have to reduce the annual total, because the business's cash flow is good. She could just adjust what she takes out to allow for seasonal fluctuations.

- The bank loan repayment is her remaining problem. The cash flow budget shows us that if Sue can find savings of around £1,500 over the year, she can just manage to make this payment at the end of December. However this may not be possible. She should talk to her bank manager, show them this information (they may be impressed with the fact that she has produced a budget) and negotiate to pay some in December and some part way through next year. Bank managers prefer not to have nasty surprises and would usually be happy to do this.

- If all else fails, she needs to ask her bank for an overdraft facility so that she does not end up paying high charges for an unexpected overdraft. She may need this in any case: just moving the ATOL and insurance payments to a different part of the year still leaves August looking vulnerable. A slight shortfall in cash inflows will push her into the red at this stage.

- Finally, don't forget that we have assumed there is no cash in the bank at the start of the year, because we had no information on this point. A few thousand pounds would make all the difference. Sue could put some of her own personal money in to tide the business over, but note that this is really not very different from suggesting that she cuts her drawings back a little bit.

'Our figures are the same as last year's, except that there are minuses where the pluses used to be'

Let's now look at a slightly more complex example. The Outdoor Centre is a business based in the Outer Hebrides which provides accommodation and activities for youth groups. To set a budget for laundry costs the managers need to estimate the number of centre users expected to use the linen provided by the centre, and multiply this by the cost of laundering to get the total expected laundry costs.

If during the year laundry costs come in lower or higher than the budget figures it means that the assumptions used by management in preparing the budget are not holding. That could have implications for other parts of the business, so managers need to find out what is causing the difference. We can explore this by thinking about the example set out below.

Example 5.1

At the Outdoor Centre, the laundry budget for the current year was set at £1,500 expense and £1,500 income, so the net amount was zero. The budget was set on the basis of 1,500 centre users staying for a total of 3,200 bed nights. Of the users about two-thirds bring sleeping bags and the remainder use centre linen. People using sleeping bags are provided with a pillowcase for free; people using centre linen are charged £3 per linen set (duvet cover, sheet and pillowcase). The agency that provides the laundry service charges £2.50 per linen set and 25p per pillowcase. The laundry charges made by the centre to linen set users are expected to cover all the laundry costs. Half-way through the year it became obvious that the expenses were going to be higher than the budgeted figure, so the centre would have to find additional funds to pay the laundry expense.

The reasons for this difference between the budget and the actual figure could be simply that there has been an error. Possibly the figures have been written down wrongly or a bill paid twice. Alternatively something else could have been mixed up with the laundry expenses, for instance cleaning materials might have been added into that heading by mistake. However, assuming that the possibility of errors has been checked and discounted, the reasons then must have something to do with users or prices. Higher prices for all or just part of the laundry would lead to this difference. Would more users have caused this problem? If there were more users and they used the linen and were charged for it in the same way as had been budgeted for the original user numbers, the income should also have risen in line with the expense.

What if the proportion of linen set users to sleeping-bag users changed? More linen set users would increase the expenses, but would increase the income by more, so the laundry part of the business would be making a profit. (For every user who forgets their sleeping bag and has to pay for linen the income goes up by £3 and the costs go up by £2.25 (£2.50 − 25p), so there would be a net increase in income of 75p per user.) Fewer linen set users and more sleeping-bag users would reduce the expenses but reduce the income by a greater amount, so there would be a need to subsidise laundry costs. (For every linen set user who brings a sleeping bag the costs go down by £2.25 (£2.50 − 25p) but income goes down by £3.00.)

What if the number of users stayed the same but the length of their stay changed? This should make no difference to laundry costs. What if the number of bed nights stayed the same but there were more individuals staying for a shorter period? More linen would be used, which would increase expense costs, but you would also expect there to be an increase in income and there was none.

So the possible causes for an increase in costs unmatched by an increase in income are a rise in the prices charged by the agency providing the laundry service and/or more people bringing sleeping bags. Both should lead to a review of the charges set for linen users and a revision of the budget for the remainder of the year and future years.

What really happened to the laundry expenses?

There was one other possible reason: the expenses that are recorded are not all for the period concerned. During the year, a bill came in which included linen that had been used and cleaned last year. This amount had not been added into last year and taken out of this year as an accrual so the total expense for the current year would never match the income charged to users. The laundry service provider was very slow to invoice, sometimes taking 15 months to send out a bill. For future years the Outdoor Centre took two courses of action. They estimated laundry costs due at the year-end from laundry delivery notes and phoned up the laundry regularly to ask for their invoice.

As you worked all the way through that example you experienced the type of investigation done by managers to work out what their figures mean. Comparing actual figures with the budget should lead to a better understanding of what is going on in the business, as should any comparison of progress against a plan.

In order to make managers more responsible for their area of the business it is common for them to be in charge of their budgets. By matching the budget control with the management control an individual can be responsible for ensuring that the budget is not overspent (for expense budgets) or under-achieved (for income budgets). Budgets should be set at a realistic level. In order to do this, the people who are most concerned with the activity in question need to be involved or consulted. Without this the budget set can be much too low for one item and/or too high for another. If the budgets are too far away from a realistic level then the comparison becomes meaningless, and the manager who is supposed to be controlling the budget has been set up to fail.

Example 5.2

A hospital had to make savings and it was decided that each cost centre had to reduce its budget by 2 per cent. Each ward was a cost centre, as were the dispensary, restaurant, physiotherapy, X-ray, outpatients, etc. By cutting 2 per cent from each budget the management felt that they had been fair to everyone. Four nurses staffed the day ward, which took in elderly people for day care. These people had worked on the ward for a long time and it was unlikely that they would leave in the near future. The ward had barely any expenses other than the staff costs. It was not possible to operate the ward safely with fewer staff on duty and if anyone were made redundant it would have cost more money as well as seriously affecting the service.

In this situation it is clearly not possible to make savings of 2 per cent. Cutting the number of nurses by one would lead to 25 per cent savings on staff costs, but it was not possible to do this for safety and operational reasons. If she had been consulted, the manager would have explained this, and perhaps she would have been able to negotiate another solution. What the manager did instead in her budget report was to retain the original budget figures as a comparison with the actual results, to highlight the small savings that she was able to achieve and to show that she was not overspending. She then showed the 'required' 2 per cent savings as a bottom line adjustment so that the budget figures she was using for comparative purposes reconciled with those imposed by central management. This also made the point that the 2 per cent saving was not realistic for the day ward budget.

5.3 Different types of costs and their impact on budgets

Costs can be split into different types to reflect the way they arise. The different types need different budget treatment. In Example 5.2 the staff costs of the nurses on the day ward are variable, or proportional costs; they are incurred in relation to the amount of time the ward is open rather than the number of patients. But because the ward hours have been fixed for a long time, and because of the political outcry if the ward hours were reduced and fewer patients treated, their costs are effectively fixed, at least in the medium term. The hospital can expect one-twelfth of the budget to be incurred each month.

The laundry costs at the Outdoor Centre in Example 5.1 are proportional to user numbers, although not directly so because of the sleeping-bag users. The budget for each month should be set in proportion to the users expected.

Costs that vary in relation to a chosen measure of activity (for example, output) are known as variable costs. Variable costs can seem fixed if they are in proportion to something that does not change frequently. However, true fixed costs are costs that do not vary in relation to the chosen measure of activity. An example might be staff costs for a supermarket. If the chosen measure of activity is monthly sales, then the costs of employing shelf-stackers is likely to be variable as they would usually be paid on an hourly basis. The costs of managerial staff would be fixed as they would be paid monthly salaries and would probably have to be given at least one month's notice of dismissal. Some costs have both fixed and variable elements, of course. For example, telephone charges normally comprise a fixed element (often described as 'line rental' or similar) and a variable element – the charges for the actual use of the service.

Apart from variable and fixed costs there are also costs that are independent of the volume of activity (like fixed costs) but are not yet committed and so can be discretionary. There are also costs for occasional events and contingencies. Paula's Pipes might regard employee costs as fixed, plumbing components as variable, new equipment as discretionary ('we could probably manage with that old wrench for another few months') and lawyer's fees as part of contingency budgets. Contingency budgets are always a problem. You hope that the event does not occur, and it is unlikely to in any one year, so should you budget for it, and how much? Insurance can cover many contingencies, including legal assistance for Paula, and effectively convert an unpredictable large expense into a predictable regular smaller expense.

Activity 5.3

Spend about **10 minutes** on this activity

Purpose: to reinforce your understanding of fixed, variable, discretionary and contingency budget types.

Task: think of a couple of examples of each type of expense budget for a local library.

Budget type	Examples
Fixed	
Variable	
Discretionary	
Contingency	

Feedback

Fixed-cost budgets could include staff costs, rates, subscriptions and non-metered water.

Variable-cost budgets, which behave proportionally, could include staff and electricity (in proportion to opening hours), metered water (in proportion to user numbers), and book repair costs (in proportion to borrowings).

Discretionary budgets could include the book purchase budget, non-urgent maintenance and children's story-time costs.

We would expect contingency budgets to be covered by insurance for employee liability, public liability and property. However, something excluded by insurance, such as an act of terrorism, might come into this category.

You should be able to see that different cost budgets, and income budgets, behave in different ways. To be able to set and monitor a budget managers need to understand how each item behaves, how it is affected by changes in business levels, and if it can be affected by the staff responsible for it. For instance the head librarian may be responsible for all the above budgets, but the amount of control possible over the budgets may vary. The money paid for rates could not be changed without changing the location of the library, a decision that would probably be made higher up the business. The same might apply to the variable costs if the hours of service to which they are related cannot be changed by the librarian.

Discretionary budgets are the easiest type to change. If there is pressure to trim costs budgets, it is simpler to cut the non-urgent maintenance budget, book budget or research and development budget than decide to change the amount of service being delivered or product being made. This is logical in a business with a short planning and budget cycle as the pressure might ease up next year. However, the long-term effects of annually trimming the discretionary budgets can result in poorly maintained assets, a lack of new developments, and less innovative products and services.

5.4 Behavioural consequences of budgets

Budgets and the budgeting process can have unanticipated behavioural consequences. One of the purposes of budgets is to motivate people, by giving them targets to work towards, and against which they will be evaluated. However, budgets can also have demotivating effects. You may be able to think of examples from businesses that you have worked for, or with which you are familiar. We made the point earlier in this study session that if budgets are set at unrealistic levels then those who are responsible for them have been set up to fail.

An example might be where a manager is given a budget for the costs of running their department, rather than being involved in setting it. If they know they are going to be evaluated according to their success or failure at staying within the budget, then they may react by trying to do just this. Alternatively, they may react by overspending in order to 'prove' that the budget was unrealistic. A further layer of complication is often added by a perception that the budget has to be spent as otherwise next year's budget will be set at a reduced level.

The next activity looks at this type of situation.

Activity 5.4

Spend about **30 minutes** on this activity

Purpose: to think about some of the behavioural implications of budgetary control.

Task: consider the following scenario, and then jot down some thoughts about the questions that follow.

Carlo is the recently appointed manager of a small sales team based at a regional office of a printing company. He has been given responsibility for his department's running costs, but has not been involved in setting the budget for these costs. He is paid a monthly salary of £1,300, but will also receive a bonus if his department's actual costs in any month are less than budgeted. The bonus is calculated as 75 per cent of the amount by which actual costs are less than budgeted (there is no penalty for exceeding the budget – but no bonus either!). It is paid the following month.

For the current financial year (January to December) the budget has been set at £10,000 a month. During January, February and March actual costs were slightly over £10,000. However, during April and May actual costs were £9,000, so Carlo received his bonus (£750 for each month). In June, Carlo heard on the office grapevine that the firm's central budget committee had decided to reduce his budget to £9,500 for the rest of the financial year.

Questions:

1   How do you think Carlo would be likely to react to this news?

2   If you were on the central budget committee, say as a newly appointed member, what suggestions might you make about this situation?

Feedback

1   Carlo is likely to be upset and angry. He probably feels he has relatively little control over some of the department's costs (though note that we do not know what these are), and he certainly wasn't involved in setting the budget. Nevertheless he has worked hard to control costs, and just as he feels he is getting a grip on things, look how he is rewarded. His basic salary is not high, and he needs that bonus. He feels like resigning.

Once he has had a chance to reflect further, other thoughts may occur to him. Gossip is not always accurate. Perhaps he had better check on this information before he resigns. There are other possibilities too. He may not have control over incurring most of the costs, but perhaps he does have some control over which month they are recorded for budgeting purposes. For example, he can possibly delay authorising payment until the following month, or he may be able to push other bills through more promptly. This would give him some flexibility. If he can see that, in a particular month, he is going to overspend his budget whatever happens, then he may as well get some other expenses paid early, so that next month there is less to be paid. This means that next month may come in under budget – and he gets his bonus. He is not penalised for overspending, so it could be worth it. By shifting costs around like this he will not change *total* costs for the year, but he may have a better chance of getting a bonus in some, if not all, months.

According to anecdotal evidence, this type of behaviour is common practice in large organisations where staff are rewarded by profit-related bonus schemes. If the senior managers know that there is going to be bad news for the shareholders (in the form of lower profits than expected), then reportedly they take the opportunity to deal with any other impending 'hits' to profit in the same accounting period. This has the effect of freeing up the following accounting period for higher profits, which pleases the shareholders, and the staff may get their bonuses too!

2   Assuming that the news about the cut in Carlo's budget is true and not just rumour, as a member of the budget committee you might be unhappy that he had heard this on the office grapevine. Carlo should have heard about it via formal channels, but large organisations often make the mistake of letting this sort of leak happen.

Cutting the budget back is an understandable reaction in a situation like this, where the manager responsible seems to have found it easy to meet the budget, but it is arguably short-sighted. It will become clear after a few more months that Carlo has decided to manipulate his costs – and if you are honest you would agree that, if you reward people in this way, you must expect this sort of reaction. Several points might occur to you:

- o   We can fix this by replacing the current scheme by one where the bonus relates to costs saved over the year taken as a whole, not just month by month. However, if Carlo is being rewarded in this way he may not be happy if he has to wait until the end of the year for his bonus.

- o   The current salary structure is part of the problem. The bonus is too high relative to Carlo's basic salary. This creates incentives for dysfunctional behaviour: if Carlo is encouraged in this way to save costs, he may begin to do this in areas where the end result will be undesirable. For example, he may refuse permission for his staff to go on training courses; this will save money in the short term, but will have longer-term effects on productivity and staff morale. A higher basic salary, with a bonus that is a genuine end-of-year reward for success at keeping costs low, but is not out of proportion to the basic salary, would be appropriate.

○ Finally, involving Carlo in setting the budget for which he has been made responsible seems a good idea.

5.5 Conclusion

This session has been devoted to some of the most useful reports prepared by accountants for use within businesses – budgets. We began by considering what budgets are, and how they are prepared. This was followed by some examples of budgets, how they are used in practice and how the information they present can help managers make decisions and take action. Then we looked at the different types of cost that need to be dealt with when budgets are prepared, and how they behave in relation to changes in the level of business activity. Finally we spent some time thinking about how budgets and budgetary control can have behavioural implications.

5.6 Learning outcomes

By the end of this study session on budgets and the budgeting process you should be able to:

- explain what a budget is, and why it can be an important tool to help owners and managers run their businesses;
- describe in outline how the budgeting process operates;
- understand the importance of classifying costs into different types according to their behaviour in relation to changes in business activity;
- appreciate the behavioural implications of budgeting.

You have developed your learning by:

- applying your learning about budgets to practical examples.

Conclusion to Book 3

The aim of Book 3 is to introduce you to some of the main concepts and terms that will be used in an accounting and finance function in any business. We hope you appreciate the central role that accounting information plays in the business decision-making process. Whether you are working in, or studying, a business, some understanding of basic accounting and finance will help you to appreciate more the activities of a business. Students are often frightened by what is often seen as a technical subject. We hope that, by using simple practical examples in this book and by situating accounting in its wider context, we have dispelled some of this apprehension.

After considering what accounting does and where it came from, we moved on to exploring different financial stakeholders and understanding how cash accounting works. We then explored the different accounting statements, what they are used for, and some of the key terms within them. You should be using the B120 Glossary regularly to ensure you can define these for yourself and see how they are relevant for a business. Stepping back and looking at the world of accounting – the accounting professional bodies and the branches of accounting – and reflecting on the image of accounting were again intended to get you to think about this function 'in the round'. As in all business functions, the activities and decisions made in accounting have a knock-on effect on all other functions. The final study session on budgets perhaps brings this to light; the need to plan and control financial resources within the business will have a direct impact on other resources and, ultimately, what the business might be able to do.

This book has provided a relatively short and general introduction to the world of accounting and finance in business. In future courses that you study you will learn about the accounting and finance techniques and issues introduced here. We hope you have both enjoyed, and feel more confident about, studying accounting and finance in business.

References

Atrill, P. and McClaney, E. (2001) *Accounting and Finance for Non-Specialists* (3rd edn), Harlow, Financial Times Prentice Hall (an imprint of Pearson Education).

BBC (1998) 'How the stars cover their assets', *BBC News*, 31 July [online] http://bbc.co.uk/1/hi/uk/142982.stm (accessed 14 March 2006).

Capon, C. (2004) *Understanding Organisational Context: Inside and Outside Organisations* (2nd edn), Harlow, Financial Times Prentice Hall (an imprint of Pearson Education).

CIMA (2000) *Management Accounting Official Terminology*, London, Chartered Institute of Management Accountants.

Day and Taylor (2002) 'SMEs: The Accounting Deficitquest', *Accountancy*, January 2002, p. 130.

Dyson, J. R. (2004) *Accounting for Non-Accounting Students* (6th edn), Harlow, Financial Times Prentice Hall (an imprint of Pearson Education).

Jacobsen, L. E. (1964) 'The ancient Inca empire of Peru and the double entry accounting concept', *Journal of Accounting Research*, Vol. 2, No. 2, pp. 221–8.

Montaner, C. A. (2000) *Twisted Roots*, pp. 117–21 [online] http://www.firmaspress.com/Twisted_Roots.pdf (accessed 19 September 2006).

Wild, D. (2002) 'The truth about bad news', *Accountancy Age*, 24 October.

Essential Reading 1

Public and private entities

The main aim of this section is to introduce you to the two main types of entities with which we shall be primarily concerned in this book: *sole traders* and *companies*. Before we can do this we need to explain a little bit about the structure of the national economy of the United Kingdom.

In order to simplify our analysis, we will assume that the UK economy can be classified into two broad groupings: the *profit-making sector* and the *not-for-profit sector*. Within each of these sectors it is then possible to distinguish a number of different types of organizations (or entities, as we have referred to them earlier). The basic structure that we shall be following in this section is illustrated in Figure R1.1. We begin by examining the profit-making sector.

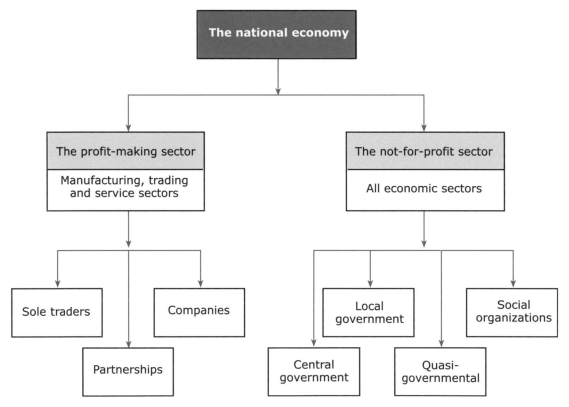

Figure R1.1 Public and private entities

The profit-making sector

The profit-making sector is extremely diverse, but it is possible to recognize three major subdivisions. These are (a) the manufacturing sector; (b) the trading sector; and (c) the service sector.

The manufacturing sector is involved in purchasing raw materials and component parts, converting (or incorporating) them into finished goods, and then selling them to customers. Examples of manufacturing enterprises include the chemicals, glass, iron and steel, and textile industries.

The trading sector purchases finished goods and then sells them to their customers without any further major conversion work normally being done on them. Trading enterprises are found in the retailing and wholesaling sectors, such as shops, supermarkets and builders' merchants.

The service sector provides advice or assistance to customers or clients, such as hairdressing, legal, and travel services. Unlike the manufacturing and trading sectors, the service sector does not usually deal in physical or tangible goods. However, there are some exceptions: the hotel and restaurant trade, for example, is normally classed as part of the service sector even though it provides major tangible services such as the provision of accommodation, food and drink.

The accounting systems required of manufacturing, trading and service sector entities are all slightly different, although they are based on similar principles and procedures. Manufacturing entity accounts are the most complex, trading entity are fairly straightforward, while service entity accounts are usually fairly simple.

Until about 15 years ago, accounting texts tended to concentrate on the manufacturing and trading sectors. This emphasis reflected the origins of nineteenth-century accounting requirements, when the manufacturing and trading sectors were of major significance. More recently, the manufacturing sector has declined in importance and the service sector has become much more significant.

...

Although there are differences in the nature of the product or the service that they offer, entities within the manufacturing, trading and service sectors may be organized on similar lines. Three main types of entities can be recognized; these are (1) *sole trader entities*; (2) *partnership entities*; and (3) *companies*. The basic distinction between such entities reflects who owns them, how they are financed, and what the law requires of them.

Sole traders

The term 'sole trader' is rather misleading for two reasons: (1) 'sole' does not necessarily mean that only one person is involved in the entity; and (2) 'trader' may also encompass manufacturing and service entities.

The term really reflects the *ownership* of the entity; the main requirement is that only one individual should own the entity. The owner would normally also be the main source of finance and he would be expected to play a reasonably active part in its management.

Sole traders usually work on a very informal basis and some private matters relating to the owner are often indistinguishable from those of the business. Sole trader accounts are fairly straightforward and there is no specific legislation that covers the accounting arrangements. ...

Partnerships

A partnership entity is very similar to a sole trader entity except that there must be at least *two owners* of the business. Partnerships sometimes grow out of a sole trader entity, perhaps because more money needs to be put into the business or because the sole trader needs some help in managing it. It is also quite common for a new business to start out as partnerships, for example when some friends get together or start a home-decorating service or to form a car-repair business.

The partners should agree among themselves how much money they will each put into the business, what jobs they will do, how many hours they will work, and how the profits and losses will be shared. In the absence of any agreement (whether formal or informal), partnerships in the United Kingdom are covered by the Partnership Act 1890.

There is also a new type of partnership. This was introduced in 2001. It is known as a *Limited Liability Partnership*. (LLP). An LLP has a separate legal personality from that of its owners (like a company), and it protects the partners from personal bankruptcy.

… Partnership accounts are very similar in principle to those of sole traders …

Companies

A company is another different type of business organization. There are many different forms of companies but generally the law regards all companies as having a separate existence from that of their owners … [Here] we are going to be primarily concerned with *limited liability companies*. The term 'limited liability' means that the owners of such companies are only required to finance the business up to an agreed amount; once they have contributed that amount, they cannot be called upon to contribute any more, even if the company gets into financial difficulties.

As there is a risk that limited liability companies may not be able to pay off their debts, Parliament has had to give some legal protection to those parties who may become involved with them. The details are contained within the Companies Act 1985. …

The not-for-profit sector

By 'not-for-profit' we mean those entities whose primary purpose is to provide a service to the public rather than to make a profit from their operations. We will consider this sector under four main headings: (1) central government; (2) local government; (3) quasi-governmental bodies; and (4) social organizations.

Within the three governmental groups, there is a wide variety of different types of entities. We do not need to consider them in any detail since governmental accounting is extremely specialized and it would require a book of its own. We shall also not be dealing with the accounts of social organizations in any great depth because their accounting procedures are similar to profit-making entities.

Central government

Central government is responsible for services such as macro-economic policy, education, defence, foreign affairs, health, and social security. These responsibilities are directly controlled by Cabinet ministers who answer to Parliament at Westminster for their actions. In 1999, some of these central government responsibilities were 'devolved', i.e. they became the direct responsibility of elected bodies in Northern Ireland, Scotland, and Wales.

Local government

For well over a century, central government has also devolved many of its responsibilities to 'local' authorities, i.e. smaller units of authority that have some geographical and community coherence. Councillors are elected by the local community. They have responsibility for those services that central government has delegated, for example, the local administration of education, housing, the police and social services.

Quasi-governmental bodies

Central government also operates indirectly through quasi-governmental bodies, such as the British Broadcasting Corporation (BBC), the Post Office, colleges and universities. Such bodies are nominally independent of central government, although their main funds are normally provided by central government and their senior managers may be appointed by government ministers.

Social organizations

The social organizations category covers a wide range of cultural, educational, recreational and social bodies. Some are formally constituted and professionally managed, such as national and international charities, while others are local organizations run by volunteers on a part-time basis, e.g. bridge and rugby clubs.

(Source: Dyson, J. R., 2004, *Accounting for Non-Accounting Students*, 6th edn, Harlow, Financial Times Prentice Hall, pp. 17–21)

Essential Reading 2

Branches of accounting

The work that accountants now undertake ranges far beyond that of simply preparing financial and costing statements. Indeed, at the beginning of the twenty-first century it can be argued that there are now five main branches of accounting and a number of important sub-branches. These various branches are shown in diagrammatic form in Figure R2.1.

...

We will deal with each of the main branches of accounting broadly in the order that they have developed over the last 100 years, i.e. financial accounting, management accounting, auditing, taxation, and financial management. Other less significant branches will be covered in one broad section after the section on financial management.

Financial accounting

... [T]he formal definition of Financial Accounting used by the Chartered Institute of Management Accountants (CIMA) ... is as follows:

> The classification and recording of the monetary transactions of an entity in accordance with established concepts, principles, accounting standards and legal requirements and their presentation, by means of profit and loss accounts, balance sheets and cash flow statements, during and at the end of an accounting period.

(Source: CIMA, 2000, quoted in Dyson, 2004, p.10)

...

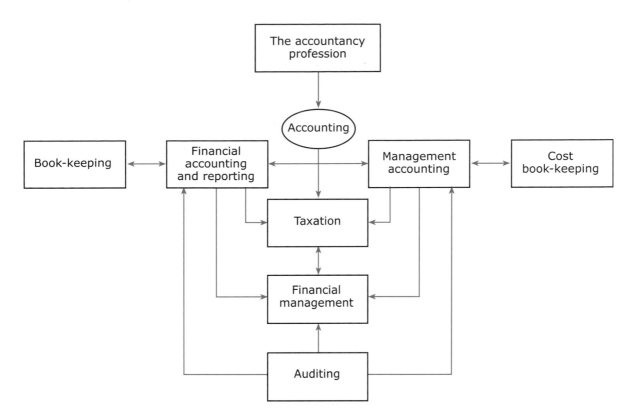

Figure R2.1 The branches of accounting

A distinction can be made between *financial accounting* and *financial reporting*. … We suggest that you regard *financial accounting* as being the accounting process that ends with the preparation of the profit and loss account, the balance sheet and the cash flow statement … *Financial reporting* is the process of communicating financial accounting to users of such information; it may involve supplying additional information and a detailed quantitative and qualitative analysis of the underlying data.

Book-keeping

An important sub-branch of financial accounting is book-keeping. Indeed, book-keeping may be regarded as the foundation upon which the entire discipline of accounting is built.

Book-keeping is a mechanical task involving the collection of basic financial data. The data are entered in special records known as *books of account,* and then extracted in the form of a trial balance. The *trial balance* enables a profit and loss account and a balance sheet to be prepared.

The CIMA definition of book-keeping is as follows:

> Recording of monetary transactions, appropriately classified, in the financial records of an entity, either by manual means, or otherwise.
>
> (CIMA, 2000)

While handwritten systems of book-keeping are still quite common, computerized ones are gradually replacing manual systems even in very small entities. Irrespective of the method used in recording data, however, the same principles still apply.

Management accounting

Until the nineteenth century there were no separate branches of accounting such as we recognize today. The accounting practised before that time was what we now call *financial accounting*. From the middle of the nineteenth century, as the UK and other countries became more industrialized (especially in the United States of America), another form of accounting became recognizable. It became known as *costing* or *cost accounting*.

… [A] separate collection and recording system was set up to provide managers with more information and more frequently than was possible with the then traditional form of accounting. Such information was needed mainly for stock valuation purposes and to work out the cost of individual products and processes. In order to meet this need a separate recording system was set up. This was known as *cost book-keeping*. Thus, we might define cost book-keeping as follows:

> The process of collecting, recording, extracting and summarizing cost data for stock valuation and product costing purposes.

While cost accounting may be defined as:

> The compilation, adaptation and reporting of cost data and information for managerial decision-making purposes.

The distinction between cost book-keeping and cost accounting is similar to that between book-keeping and financial accounting/reporting.

During the twentieth century separate book-keeping and cost book-keeping systems were gradually abandoned, but stock valuation and product costing continued to be the two main functions of a cost accounting system. However, as the century developed accountants were called upon to supply managers with accounting and cost information for some additional purposes. These included information for planning and control, and information for decision-making. Such functions meant that cost accounting had increased its boundaries and it was no longer confined to dealing with historical data. Planning and decision-making, for example, primarily looks towards the future while cost accounting is based very much on the past.

The term 'cost accounting' was, therefore, no longer appropriate to describe a much wider range of functions and the much broader description of 'management accounting' has taken its place. Hence, cost accounting is now regarded as being merely a branch of *management accounting*.

The formal definition of management accounting given by CIMA is as follows:

The application of the principles of accounting and financial management to create, protect, preserve and increase value so as to deliver that value to stakeholders of profit and not-for-profit enterprises, both public and private. (CIMA 2000)

...

Auditing

We may define auditing as:

An examination and assessment of the activities, controls, records and systems that underpin accounting information.

Not all entities have their accounts audited but for some organizations (such as large limited liability companies) it is a legal requirement.

Auditors are often trained accountants who specialize in ascertaining whether the accounts are credible, i.e. whether they can be believed. There are two main types of auditors. They are as follows.

1 *External auditors*. External auditors are appointed by the owners of an entity. They are independent of the entity and they are not employed by it. They report to the owners and not to the managers of the entity. Large limited liability companies are required to have an external audit. External auditors are responsible for ensuring that the financial accounts represent what is called 'a true and fair view' of the entity's affairs for a certain period of time. They may do some detailed checking of its records in order to be able to come to such a view but normally they would be selective. If they are then satisfied, they will be able to report their findings to the owners. The public often believe that the job of an auditor is to discover whether any fraud has taken place. This is not so
...

2 *Internal auditors*. Some entities employ internal auditors. Internal auditors are appointed by the managers of the entity; they are employees of the entity and they answer to its management. Internal auditors perform routine tasks and undertake some detailed checking of the entity's accounting procedures. Their task may also go beyond the financial accounts; for example, they may do some checking of the planning and control procedures and conduct 'value-for-money' tests.

External auditors and internal auditors usually work very closely together. Nevertheless, they do have separate roles and responsibilities. External auditors have always to remember that internal auditors are employees of the entity; they may be strongly influenced by the management of the entity and they may be subject to the pressures of other employees, e.g. job security, pay, and promotion prospects.

External auditors also do not enjoy complete independence. In the case of a large company, for example, the directors (i.e. the managers) will appoint them and, in practice, dismiss them. It is possible for the auditors to appeal directly to the shareholders but the shareholders usually accept the directors' recommendations.

Taxation

Taxation is a highly complex and technical branch of accounting. Those accountants who are involved in tax work are responsible for computing the amount of tax payable by both business entities and individuals. It is not necessary for anybody or any entity to pay more tax than is required by the law. It is, therefore, perfectly legitimate to search out all legal means of minimizing the amount of tax that might be demanded by the Government. This is known as *tax avoidance*. The non-declaration [of] sources of income on which tax might be payable is known as *tax evasion*. Tax evasion is a very serious offence and it can lead to a long prison sentence. In practice, the borderline between tax avoidance and tax evasion is a narrow one and tax accountants have to steer a fine line between what is lawful and what might not be acceptable.

Financial management

Financial management is a relatively new branch of accounting. It has grown rapidly over the last 30 years. Financial managers are responsible for setting financial objectives, making plans based on those objectives, obtaining the finance needed to achieve the plans, and generally safeguarding all the financial resources of the entity.

Financial managers are much more likely to be heavily involved in the *management* of an entity than is generally the case with other management accountants (although that is changing). It should also be noted that financial managers draw on a much wider range of disciplines (e.g. economics and mathematics) than does the more traditional accountant, and they also rely more heavily on non-financial and more qualitative data.

Other branches

The main branches of accounting described above cannot always be put into such neat categories. Accountants in practice (that is, those who work from an office and offer their services to the public, like a solicitor) usually specialize in auditing, financial accounting or taxation. Most accountants working in commerce, industry or the public sector will be employed as management accountants, although some may deal specifically with auditing, financial accounting or taxation matters.

One other highly specialist branch of accounting that you may sometimes read about is that connected with *insolvency*, i.e. with bankruptcy or liquidation. *Bankruptcy* is a formal legal procedure. The term is applied to individuals when their financial affairs are so serious that they have to be given some form of legal protection from their creditors. The term *liquidation* is usually applied to a company when it also gets into serious financial difficulties and its affairs have to be 'wound up' (that is, arranged for it to go out of existence in an orderly fashion).

Companies do not necessarily go immediately into liquidation if they get into financial difficulties. An attempt will usually be made either to rescue them or to protect certain types of creditors. In these situations, accountants sometimes act as *administrators*. Their appointment freezes creditors' rights. This prevents the company from being put into liquidation during a period when the administrators are attempting to manage the company. By contrast, *receivers* may be appointed on behalf of loan creditors. The creditors' loans may be secured on certain property, and the receivers will try to obtain the income from that property, or they may even attempt to sell it.

…

The accountancy profession

There is nothing to stop anyone in the United Kingdom calling himself or herself an accountant, and setting up in business as an accountant. However, some accounting work is restricted (such as the auditing of large limited liability companies) unless the accountant holds a recognized qualification. Indeed, accountants are sometimes described as being *qualified accountants*. This term is usually applied to someone who is a member of one of the major accountancy bodies (although many 'non-qualified' accountants would strongly dispute that they were not equally 'qualified'[ )]. There are six major accountancy bodies operating in the United Kingdom and they are as follows:

1   Institute of Chartered Accountants in England and Wales (ICAEW);

2   Institute of Chartered Accountants in Ireland (ICAI);

3   Institute of Chartered Accountants of Scotland (ICAS);

4   Association of Chartered Certified Accountants (ACCA);

5   Chartered Institute of Management Accountants (CIMA);

6   Chartered Institute of Public Finance and Accountancy (CIPFA).

The Irish Institute (ICAI) is included in the above list because it has a strong influence in Northern Ireland.

The organization of the accountancy profession is also shown in Figure R2.2.

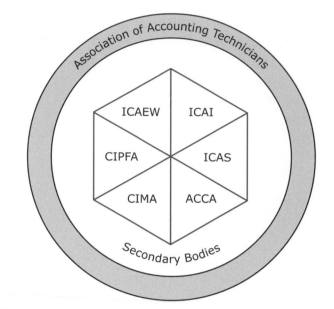

Key

ICAEW   Institute of Chartered Accountants in England and Wales
ICAI   Institute of Chartered Accountants in Ireland
ICAS   Institute of Chartered Accountants of Scotland
ACCA   Association of Chartered Certified Accountants
CIMA   Chartered Institute of Management Accountants
CIPFA   Chartered Institute of Public Finance and Accountancy

Figure R2.2 Organization of the accountancy profession in the UK

Although all of the six major professional accountancy bodies now have a Royal Charter, it is still customary to refer only to members of ICAEW, ICAI, and ICAS as *chartered accountants*. Such chartered accountants have usually had to undergo a period of training in a practising office, i.e. one that offers accounting services directly to the public. This distinguishes them from members of the other three accountancy bodies. Much practice work is involved in auditing and taxation but, after qualifying, many chartered accountants go to work in commerce or industry. ACCA members may also obtain their training in practice, but relevant experience elsewhere counts towards their qualification. CIMA members usually train and work in industry, while CIPFA members specialize almost exclusively in central and local government.

Apart from the six major bodies, there are a number of important (although far less well-known) smaller accountancy associations and societies, e.g. the Association of Authorised Public Accountants, the Institute of Company Accountants, and the Institute of Cost and Executive Accountants. Such bodies offer some form of accountancy qualification but they have not yet managed to achieve the status or prestige attached to being a member of one of the six major bodies. Hence, they are referred to as *secondary bodies*.

There is also another very important accountancy body, known as the Association of Accounting Technicians. The Association was formed in 1980 as a professional organization especially for those accountants who *assist* qualified accountants in preparing accounting information. In order to become an accounting technician, it is necessary to take (or be exempt from) the Association's examinations. These are not easy, although they tend to be less technically demanding and more practical than those of the six major bodies.

(Source: Dyson, 2004, *Accounting for Non-Accounting Students*, 6th edn, Harlow, Financial Times Prentice Hall, pp. 10–16)

Essential Reading 3

Budgeting and budgetary control

We start our analysis by establishing what we mean by a 'budget' and 'budgetary control'.

Budget

The term *budget* is usually well understood by the layman. Many people, for example, often prepare a quite sophisticated budget for their own household expenses. In fact, albeit in a very informal sense, everyone does some budgeting at some time or other, even if it is only by making a rough comparison between the next month's salary and the next month's expenditure. Such a budget may not be very precise, and it may not be formally written down. Nevertheless, it contains all the ingredients of what accountants mean by a budget. The essential features of a formal budget may be summarized as follows:

1 *Policies*. A budget is based on the policies needed to fulfil the objectives of the entity.

2 *Data*. Quantitative data contained in a budget are usually translated into monetary terms.

3 *Documentation*. Details of a budget are normally contained within a formal written document.

4 *Period*. Budget details will refer to a defined future period of time.

In practice, a considerable number of budgets would be prepared. In a manufacturing entity, for example, these will include sales, production and administration budgets. These budgets would then be combined into an overall budget known as a *master budget*, comprising (a) a budgeted profit and loss account; (b) a budgeted balance sheet; and (c) a budgeted cash flow statement.

Once a master budget had been prepared, it would be closely examined to see whether the overall plan could be accommodated. It might be the case, for example, that the sales budget indicated a large increase in sales. This may have required the production budgets to be prepared on the basis of this extra sales demand. However, the cash budget might have suggested that the entity could not meet the extra sales and production activity that would be required. In these circumstances, additional financing arrangements may have had to be made, because obviously no organization would normally turn down the opportunity of increasing its sales.

In practice, the preparation of individual budgets can be a useful exercise even if nothing further is then done about them, since the exercise forces management to look ahead. It is a natural human tendency to be always looking back, but past experience is not always a guide for the future. If managers are asked to produce a budget, it encourages them to examine what they have done in relation to what they *could* do. However, the full benefits of a budgeting system are only realized when it is also used for control purposes, i.e. by the constant comparison of actual results with budgeted results, and then taking any necessary corrective action. This leads us on to consider in a little more detail what we mean by 'budgetary control'.

...

Budgetary control

In simple terms *budgetary control* involves comparing the actual results for a period with the budget for that period. If there are any differences (known as *variances*) that need attention, then corrective action will be taken to ensure that future results will conform to the budget. Budgetary control has several important features. These are as follows:

1 *Responsibilities*. Managerial responsibilities are clearly defined.

2 *Action plan*. Individual budgets lay down a detailed plan of action for a particular sphere of responsibility.

3 *Adherence*. Managers have a responsibility to adhere to their budgets once the budgets have been approved.

4 *Monitoring*. The actual performance is constantly monitored and compared with the budgeted results.

5 *Correction*. Corrective action is taken if the actual results differ significantly from the budget.

6 *Approval*. Departures from budget are only permitted if they have been approved by senior management.

7 *Variances*. Variances that are unaccounted for are subject to individual investigation.

Any variance that occurs should be carefully investigated. The current actual performance will be immediately brought back into line with the budget if it is considered necessary. Sometimes the budget itself will be changed, e.g. if there is an unexpected increase in sales. Such changes may, of course, have an effect on the other budgets, and so it cannot be done in isolation.

Now that we have outlined the nature and purpose of budgeting and budgetary control, we are in a position to investigate how the system works.

Procedure

The budget *procedure* starts with an examination of the entity's objectives. These may be very simple. They may include, for example, an overall wish to maximize profits, to foster better relations with customers, or to improve the working conditions of employees. Once an entity has decided upon its overall objectives, it is in a position to formulate some detailed plans.

These will probably start with a *forecast*. Note that there is a technical difference between a forecast and a budget. A forecast is a prediction of what is *likely* to happen, whereas a budget is a carefully prepared plan of what *should* happen.

In order to make it easier for us to guide you through the budgeting process, we will examine each stage individually. We do so below and the procedure is also depicted in Figure R3.1. We will be dealing with a manufacturing entity in the private sector. The budgeting procedures for service sector entities are similar but not as complicated. Budgets in the public sector (such as in local government) involve a different procedure.

The budget period

The main budget period is usually based on a calendar year. It could be shorter or longer depending upon the nature of the product cycle; for example, the fashion industry may adopt a short budget period of less than a year, while the construction industry may choose (say) a five-year period. Irrespective of the industry, however, a calendar year is usually a convenient period to choose as the base period, because it fits in with the financial accounting period.

Besides determining the main budget period, it is also necessary to prepare sub-period budgets. Sub-period budgets are required for budgetary control purposes, since the actual results have to be frequently compared with the budgeted results. The sub-budget periods for some activities may need to be very short if tight control is to be exercised over them. The cash budget, for example, may need to be compiled on a weekly basis, whereas the administration budget may only need to be prepared quarterly.

Administration

The budget procedure may be administered by a special budget committee, or it may be supervised by the accounting function. It will be necessary for the budget committee to lay down general guidelines in accordance with the entity's objectives, and to ensure that individual departments do not operate completely independently. The production department, for example, will need to know what the entity is budgeting to sell so that it can prepare its own budget on the basis of those sales. However, the detailed production budget must still remain the entire responsibility of the production manager.

The budget period	How long?
Budget administration	Who is involved?
The budgeting process	What budgets?

Figure R3.1 The budgeting procedure

This procedure is in line with the concept of responsibility accounting ... If the control procedure is to work properly, managers must be given responsibility for a clearly defined area of activity, such as a cost centre. Thereafter, they are fully answerable for all that goes on there. Unless managers are given complete authority to act within clearly defined guidelines, they cannot be expected to account for something that is outside their control. This means that, as far as budgets are concerned, managers must help prepare, amend and approve their own responsibility centre's budget; otherwise, the budgetary control system will not work.

...

The budgeting process

The budgeting process is illustrated in Figure R3.2. Study the figure very carefully, noting how the various budgets fit together.

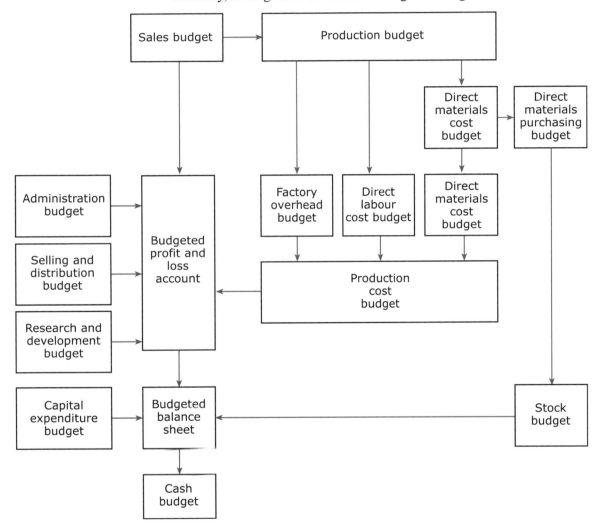

Figure R3.2 The interrelationship of budgets

...

In commercial organizations, the first budget to be prepared is usually the sales budget. Once the sales for the budget period (and for each sub-budget period) have been determined, the next stage is to calculate the effect on production. This will then enable an agreed level of activity to be determined. The *level of activity* may be expressed in so many units, or as a percentage of the theoretical productive capacity of the entity. Once it has been established, departmental managers can be instructed to prepare their budgets on the basis of the required level of activity.

Let us assume, for example, that 1000 units can be sold for a particular budget period. The production department manager will need this information in order to prepare his budget. This does not necessarily mean that he will budget for a production level of 1000 units, because he will also have to allow for the budgeted level of opening and closing stocks.

The budgeted production level will then be translated into how much material and labour will be required to meet that particular level. Similarly, it will be necessary to prepare overhead budgets. Much of the general overhead expenditure of the entity (such as factory administrative costs, head office costs, and research and development expenditure) will tend to be fixed, as such overheads will not be directly affected by production levels. However, in some instances a marked change in activity may lead to a change in fixed costs.

The sales and distribution overhead budget may be the one overhead budget that will not be entirely fixed in nature. An increase in the number of units sold, for example, may involve additional delivery costs.

Not all entities start the budget process with sales. A local authority usually prepares a budget on the basis of what it is likely to spend. The total budgeted expenditure is then compared with the total amount of council tax (after allowing for other income) needed to cover it. If the political cost of an increase in council tax appears too high then the council will require a reduction in the budgeted expenditure. Once the budget has been set, and the tax has been levied on that basis, departments have to work within the budgets laid down. However, since the budget will have been prepared on an estimate of the actual expenditure for the last two or three months of the old financial year, account has to be taken of any surplus or shortfall expected in the current year. If the estimate eventually proves excessive, the local authority will have overtaxed. This means that it has got some additional funds available to cushion the current year's expenditure. Of course, if it has undertaxed for any balance brought forward, departments might have to start cutting back on what they thought they could spend.

This process is quite different from the private sector, in which the budgeted sales effectively determine all the other budgets. In a local authority, it is the expenditure budgets that determine what the council tax should be, and it is only the control exercised by central government and by the local authority itself that places a ceiling on what is spent.

Functional budgets

A budget prepared for a particular department, cost centre or other identifiable sphere of responsibility is known as a *functional budget*. All the functional budgets will then be combined into the *master budget*. The master budget is, in effect, a combined budgeted profit and loss account, a budgeted balance sheet and a budgeted cash flow statement.

An initial draft of the master budget may not be acceptable to the senior management of the entity. This may be because the entity cannot cope with that particular budgeted level of activity, e.g. as a result of production or cash constraints. Indeed, one of the most important budgets is the *cash budget.* The cash budget translates all the other functional budgets (including that for capital expenditure) into cash terms. It will show in detail the pattern of cash inputs and outputs for the main budget period, as well as for each sub-budget period. If it shows that the entity will have difficulty in financing a particular budgeted level of activity (or if there is going to be a period when cash is exceptionally tight), the management will have an opportunity to seek out alternative sources of finance.

This latter point illustrates the importance of being aware of future commitments, so that something can be done in advance if there are likely to be constraints (irrespective of their nature). The master budget usually takes so long to prepare, however, that by the time it has been completed it will be almost impossible to make major alterations. It is then tempting for senior management to make changes to the functional budgets without referring them back to individual cost-centre managers. It is most unwise to make changes in this way, because it is then difficult to use such budgets for control purposes. If managers have not agreed to the changes, they will argue that they can hardly take responsibility for budgets that have been imposed on them.

(Source: Dyson, 2004, *Accounting for Non-Accounting Students*,6th edn, Harlow, Financial Times Prentice Hall, pp. 377–82)

Acknowledgements

Grateful acknowledgement is made to the following sources for permission to reproduce material in this book:

Text

Example 3.1: 'How the stars cover their assets', *BBC News Online*, 31 July 1998; *Example 4.4*: Wild, D., 'The truth about bad news', *Accountancy Age*, 24 October 2002. © 2006 VNU Business Publications Ltd. Posted with permission from Accountancy Age, contact Wright's Reprints at 877-652-5295; *Example 4.5 including Fig 4.1*: Dyson, J. R. (2004) *Accounting for Non-Accounting Students*, Pearson Education Limited, © Pearson Education Limited 2001, 2004; *Essential Readings 1, 2 and 3*: Dyson, J. R. (2004) *Accounting for Non-Accounting Students*, Pearson Education Limited, © Pearson Education Limited 2001, 2004.

Tables

Table 1.1: Capon, C. (2004) *Understanding Organisational Context: Inside and Outside Organisations*, Pearson Education Limited, © Pearson Education Limited 2000, 2004.

Figure

Figure 1.1: Dyson, J. R. (2004) *Accounting for Non-Accounting Students*, Pearson Education Limited, © Pearson Education Limited 2001, 2004.

Photographs/Illustrations

Pages 10, 13, 20, 44, 70 and 91: © REX FEATURES; *Pages 24 and 54*: © Randy Glasbergen; *Pages 36 and 85*: © Ted Goff; *Page 39*: © Stockfolio/ Alamy; *Page 56*: © www.CartoonStock.com *Page 76*: © David Sanger photography/Alamy.

Cover

Front cover image: © PhotoDisc Images.

Module team

B120 team

Dr Anja Schaefer
Dr Nik Winchester
Dr Warren Smith
Dr Vira Krakhmal
Barry Jones, *Curriculum Manager*
Carey Stephens
Susan Hughes
Rosie McGookin
Val O'Connor, *Course Team Assistant*

Original course team

Dr Diane Preston, *Course Team Chair*
Patricia McCarthy, *Course Manager*

Other contributors

Professor Judy Day
Dr Lorna J. Eller
Mick Fryer
Jonathan Winship

External examiner

Kate Greenan, *Professor of Management Education and Head of School of Accounting, Ulster University*

Developmental testers

Linda Fisher
Adam Messer
John Messer
Marina Ramtohul

Critical readers

Patricia Coffey, *Senior Lecturer, University of Brighton Business School*
Clare Cromarty, *OUBS Associate Lecturer*
Patricia Dawson, *Principal Lecturer, Thames Valley University, retired*
Helen Higson, *Director of Undergraduate Studies, Aston Business School*
Beverly Leeds, *Principal Lecturer, University of Central Lancashire*
Jill Mordaunt, *OUBS Senior Lecturer*
Paul Ranford, *OUBS Associate Lecturer*
Nigel Walton, *OUBS Associate Lecturer*

Production team

Martin Brazier, *Graphic Designer*
Angela Davies, *Media Assistant*
Richard Dobson, *Editor*
Hannah Eiseman-Renyard, *Editor*
Diane Hopwood, *Rights Assistant*
Lee Johnson, *Media Project Manager*
Siggy Martin, *Assistant Print Buyer*
Katy Nyaaba, *Media Assistant*
Jill Somerscales, *Editor*

The original production team

Jill Alger, *Editor*
Martin Brazier, *Graphic Designer*
Lene Connolly, *Print Buyer*
Sarah Cross, *Assistant Print Buyer*
Julie Fletcher, *Media Project Manager*
Diane Hopwood, *Picture Researcher*
Kate Hunter, *Editor*
Jon Owen, *Graphic Artist*
Deana Plummer, *Picture Researcher*
Jill Somerscales, *Editor*